# my **revisi⏻n** notes

# OCR GCSE
# PE

John Honeybourne

HODDER
EDUCATION
AN HACHETTE UK COMPANY

The author and publishers would like to thank the following for the use of photography in this volume:

Figure 6.1 © Paco Ayala – Fotolia; Figure 8.1 © Johnny Lye - Fotolia.com; Figure 12.1 © Warren Goldswain – Fotolia; Figure 13.1 © Shuva Rahim – Fotolia; Figure 15.1 © Michael Chamberlin – Fotolia; Figure 19.1 © Vladislav Gajic – Fotolia; Figure 20.1 © Ady Kerry / Alamy; Figure 24.1 © Sly – Fotolia.

Every effort has been made to trace and acknowledge ownership of copyright. The publishers will be glad to make suitable arrangements with any copyright holders whom it has not been possible to contact.

*Orders*

Bookpoint Ltd, 130 Milton Park, Abingdon, Oxon OX14 4SB

Telephone: (44) 01235 827720

Fax: (44) 01235 400454

Lines are open from 9.00–5.00, Monday to Saturday, with a 24 hour message answering service. You can also order through our website www.hoddereducation.co.uk

If you have any comments to make about this, or any of our other titles, please send them to educationenquiries@hodder.co.uk

*British Library Cataloguing in Publication Data*

A catalogue record for this title is available from the British Library

ISBN 9781444157451

Published 2012

| Impression number | 10 9 8 7 6 5 4 3 2 1 |
| --- | --- |
| Year | 2016, 2015, 2014, 2013, 2012 |

Hachette UK's policy is to use papers that are natural, renewable and recyclable products and made from wood grown in sustainable forests. The logging and manufacturing processes are expected to conform to the environmental regulations of the country of origin.

Illustrations by Stephanie Strickland

Typeset by Integra, India

Printed in Spain for Hodder Education, An Hachette UK Company, 338 Euston Road, London NW1 3BH

# Get the most from this book

This book will help you revise Units B451 and B453 of the OCR GCSE PE specification. You can use the contents list on pages 2 and 3 to plan your revision, topic by topic. Tick each box when you have:

1 revised and understood a topic

2 tested yourself

You can also keep track of your revision by ticking off each topic heading through the book. You may find it helpful to add your own notes as you work through each topic.

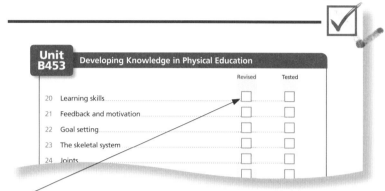

**Tick to track your progress**

### Exam tips

Throughout the book there are exam tips that explain how you can boost your final grade.

### Link to the textbook

For further information on a topic, this feature shows you where to look in the main textbook, *OCR PE for GCSE*.

**Practical examples are picked out in bold throughout the book.**

### Remember

Useful tips to help you get the most out of your revision.

### Check your understanding

Use these questions at the end of each section to make sure that you have understood every topic.

# Contents and revision planner

# 1. Key concepts

*relationship between skills, selection & application of skills, tactics & compositional ideas & the readiness of body and mind to cope with physical activity.*

## 1.1 Competence

Revised

Competence involves the **skills** you learn and how you **apply** them to physical activities and also how **ready you are** in body and mind to perform these skills in physical activities.

To be competent in physical activities, you need to:

● have learned the appropriate skills – **for example, in hockey you need to learn how to stop and hit a ball.**

● know when to use these skills – **for example, in basketball to know when to shoot.**

● use appropriate tactics in the activity – **for example, in football to know when to concentrate on attacking and when to put your efforts into defending.**

● use ideas to link movements together – **for example, in a gymnastics routine.**

● be fit enough to do the activity effectively – **for example, you should not get out of breath too easily when playing a team game.**

● have the right mental approach – **for example, in an exercise class you need to show determination to finish the class.**

> **Remember**
> SAR:
> ● Skill
> ● Apply
> ● Readiness.

> **Exam tip**
> Learn the definition and be able to give a practical example.

## 1.2 Performance

Revised

This is producing effective outcomes when participating in physical activities.

*using physical competence, understanding & knowledge of physical activity to produce ~~effective~~ effective outcomes when participating in PA.*

The concept of performance in physical education is about:

● performing well, needing to be physically able and having good skills – **for example, if you are in the school netball team then you would probably be able to run fast over a short distance and change direction well.**

● needing to know what is required in order to perform your skills well – **for example, if you are in the school football team you would read the game well and be able to make appropriate runs at the right time.**

> **Remember**
> Performance = outcomes.

## 1.3 Creativity

Revised

This is about exploring and experimenting with techniques, tactics and ideas in order to do well in physical activities.

The concept of creativity in physical education is concerned with:

● using your imagination and trying things out before deciding the best course of action – **for example, you might try different techniques in the long jump, and when you find the technique that suits your own abilities, then you will try practising that technique to be successful.**

> **Remember**
> Creativity = exploring and experimenting.

*exploring & experimenting with techniques, tactics & compositional ideas to produce efficient & effective outcomes.*

- you might try different tactics in badminton to see which one is the most effective and scores the most points – **for example, by playing close to the net or at the back of the court.**

## 1.4 Healthy, active lifestyles

Revised ☐

This is about understanding the purpose of physical activity in making us healthy.

The concept of healthy, active lifestyles is about:

- understanding the link between physical activity and a healthy lifestyle. **For example, if you participate regularly in a team sport like hockey you are more likely to be healthy.**

- understanding that if you exercise or participate regularly then this may help you not only to become fitter in your body but also to be happier in yourself.

*understanding the positive contribution, regular fit for perpose PA makes to the physical & mental health of an individual.*

**Remember**

Healthy, active lifestyle = understanding.

## Check your understanding

Tested ☐

1  The following are aspects of creativity as a physical education concept: expressing ideas; solving problems; exploring tactics; being effective.

   Describe, using practical examples, how each of the above can be achieved. *(4 marks)*

2  One of the key concepts in physical education is creativity. Which one of the following is an example of creativity in physical education?

   **a)** Participating in different physical activities.

   **b)** Thinking of new movements in a gymnastic sequence.

   **c)** Being tested on physical fitness.

   **d)** Learning fundamental motor skills. *(1 mark)*

3  Which one of the following shows how physical activity can lead to a healthy, active lifestyle?

   **a)** Playing a sport encourages you to give up smoking.

   **b)** Being a referee gives you more power.

   **c)** Joining a netball team will make you more aggressive.

   **d)** Volunteering to run a team will be financially rewarding. *(1 mark)*

# 2. Fundamental motor skills

- Fundamental motor skills are skills such as throwing, catching and running.
- These skills are important because they provide the basis for other skills.
- These essential skills also help us to follow a lifestyle that is healthy.

## 2.1 Running
Revised

- This is often developed during the toddler years and is the basis of many types of physical activities.
- Running can be analysed through technique – the type of style the participant uses to run.

Running assessment:

- Assessment of running is often through timing.
- In sport it may be over a specific distance – **for example, 100 metres or a marathon of over 26 miles.**

## 2.2 Throwing
Revised

- Throwing is also crucial in activities such as athletics – **for example, in throwing the javelin.**
- Learning the proper throwing technique will go a long way towards avoiding injuring someone and increasing distance thrown.
- The throwing action can, of course, be transferred to a number of different activities – **for example, in tennis the serve involves a throwing action.**

Throwing assessment:

- Assessment of throwing is often through measuring the distance of the object thrown.

## 2.3 Jumping
Revised

- Jumping as a fundamental motor skill is an event in its own right – **for example, long jump or high jump.**
- Jumping is also a basic requirement for many physical activities and sports.

Jumping assessment:

- Assessment of jumping is often through measuring the height or distance of the jump.
- The style of the jump may also be assessed – **for example, if performing a creative dance or gymnastic routine.**

## 2.4 Kicking
Revised

- The correct technique and accuracy are the most important elements of this action.

- Football kicking techniques include basic shooting and passing skills, up to advanced techniques, such as bending the ball around a wall and overhead kicks.
- Kicking is also important in activities such as rugby – **for example, in trying to score by kicking the ball between two upright posts and over a horizontal bar to score points.**

Kicking assessment:

- Assessment of kicking is mostly by accuracy of the kick as well as the distance travelled by the ball being kicked – **for example, successful passes or scoring goals in football.**

**Exam tip**

The specification demands that you are able to describe these fundamental skills and also to show how each can be measured and analysed. Use your practical lessons experience to help you with these descriptions.

## 2.5 Catching

Revised

- Catching is important to 'catch an opponent out' – **for example, in rounders and cricket to catch the batswoman out.**
- Many playground activities involve catching and this is often where young people learn different ways to catch a ball.

Catching assessment:

- Assessment of catching is mostly about whether a ball is caught and not dropped from the hands for a few moments.

## 2.6 Hitting

Revised

- Practical examples of hitting include in cricket with the bat, in rounders with a bat and in tennis with a racket.
- Hitting involves the use of a hitting implement – usually some sort of bat or racket. The action of hitting often involves good coordination.

Hitting assessment:

- Hitting is often assessed by how far you can hit a ball as well as the accuracy of your hit – **for example, hitting the ball in hockey can be assessed by accuracy – did you pass the ball accurately to a fellow player?**
- Hitting is an important part of contact activities – **for example, boxing**.

↑ Figure 2.1 Hitting is a fundamental motor skill.

## Check your understanding

Tested

1  Which one of the following fundamental motor skills is a main feature in playing golf? *(1 mark)*

   a) Throwing

   b) Hitting

   c) Catching

   d) Running

2  Identify **four** fundamental motor skills and describe how they are measured. *(4 marks)*

3  Which one of the following is a fundamental motor skill? *(1 mark)*

   a) Short serve in badminton

   b) Spin forehand in table tennis

   c) Running for the ball in netball

   d) A step-over in football

# 3. Decision making in physical activities

● For this topic area you need to be able to identify different types of decision making in different physical activities.

● For this topic you also need to give examples of decision making that might be made by people in the following roles:

  ● Performers

  ● Coaches or leaders

  ● Officials.

## 3.1 Different types of decision making in physical activities

Revised

● Football as a performer – **for example, deciding whether to pass to another player or to shoot.**

● Netball as a performer – **for example, deciding whether to dodge left or right around an opponent.**

● Golf as a performer – **for example, deciding on which golf club to use to hit the ball.**

● Gymnast as a performer – **for example, deciding upon a type of vault to use to score points.**

## 3.2 Decision making in different roles

Revised

As a participant:

● As a participant in a physical activity – **for example, in an exercise class or your chosen sport you will play a role.**

● That role might be to *follow the instructions from the class tutor* or in a sport it might be *to score as many goals as possible* or to *be the captain.* The decisions you make might be related to tactics or individual skills. **For example, you may choose to mark your opponent closely in basketball rather than to mark space or a zone.**

As a coach or leader:

● You could be a coach of a sports team or an individual athlete – **an example of a coach making a decision might be to decide which players to pick for a football match.**

● You could be a fitness instructor or the leader of an exercise class – **a fitness instructor might decide which main muscle groups to work.**

● You could be captain of your sports team – **a captain may decide to make a substitution.**

● You could be responsible for teaching a group or assisting teaching a group in a physical activity – **a sports leader might decide which small practice games to set up.**

As an official:

● Being an official might mean that you referee a game.

● An official could be a judge in a gymnastics competition.

● It can also mean that you help to organise a competition or physical activity.

An example of an official in football:

● **The referee, with a whistle, takes charge of a match, with the help of two assistant referees. In professional matches, a fourth official is also involved.**

● **The referee enforces the laws of the game, awarding free-kicks if there is any foul play and keeping a check on the time.**

● **The ref can also postpone, stop, suspend or call off a match if there are weather or crowd problems.**

**Exam tip**

Learn examples of decisions for every role: performer; coach or leader; official. Read the exam question carefully to check which role, if any, is being referred to.

● **The assistant referee helps out with decisions such as throw-ins and offsides and sometimes will have a better view of incidents than the referee.**

● **The fourth official is based on the touchline, assisting with substitutions and keeping a check on the managers.**

↑ **Figure 3.1 A referee is an example of the role of official in sport.**

## Check your understanding

Tested

1 Decision making is an important key process in physical education.

Describe **two** examples of decisions that might be made in each of the following roles:

**a)** Performer

**b)** Coach or leader

**c)** Official                                          *(4 marks)*

2 Which of the following is a typical decision that is made by a coach in a physical activity?                *(1 mark)*

**a)** Decide to make a substitution in a football match.

**b)** Decide when to catch the ball in a cricket match.

**c)** Decide when to pass the ball in a hockey match.

**d)** Decide to try hard during a circuit-training session.

# 4. Abiding by the rules, etiquette and sportsmanship

## 4.1 The importance of abiding by the rules

Revised

- The rules and regulations related to physical activities have been designed to protect individuals who participate, lead or officiate.
- If the laws, regulations and guidelines are followed properly and checked thoroughly then it is much less likely that an accident will occur and people's lives be put at risk.
- Rules also allow the activity to be played fairly by including boundaries of behaviour that involve mutual respect and protect all participants' well-being.
- Rules and regulations also make the game much more enjoyable because all those involved know what the boundaries are regarding what they can and cannot do.

> **Exam tip**
>
> Examiners want you to understand why rules exist in physical activities and to be able to give some examples from a variety of physical activities, along with the penalties involved for breaking these rules.
>
> - If rules are broken then in most physical activities there are consequences.
> - In many physical activities there are consequences, such as losing territory or being sent off, and in other activities it may involve being fined or even taken to court.

## 4.2 Etiquette and sportsmanship

Revised

- Etiquette involves codes of behaviour to complement the rules and regulations of a physical activity.
- In sport this is often viewed as and known as sportsmanship.

### Examples of etiquette/sportsmanship

- *Always applaud the new batsman in cricket. No matter whether you're playing for your school or your country, it's good etiquette to clap the new batsman making their way to the wicket.*
- If you compete in a physical activity it is often good etiquette or sportsmanship *to shake your opponent's hand before and after the event.*
- If you accidentally hurt or injure an opponent you would show good sportsmanship by *stopping to check whether they are okay rather than continuing the game, for example, in rugby.*
- In exercise generally there are good manners in using facilities and equipment. *For example if you are working out in a gymnasium you return the free-weights back to the containing rack after you have used them.*
- If you use exercise equipment then it is good manners or etiquette to *towel down the machine that you have been using so as to remove your sweat.*
- *Shake hands with your opponent.*
- *Thank anyone who has been participating with you or against you.*
- *Show concern for others especially when they are injured or under stress.*
- *Never swear or be abusive.*
- *Do not stretch the rules to take advantage over someone else.*

> **Exam tip**
>
> Examiners will not test you on the differences between etiquette and sportsmanship because the differences are so subtle and many people use both these terms to mean the same thing.
>
> What they *will* require is for you to:
> - be able to define what is meant by etiquette or sportsmanship
> - state why they are important
> - be able to give some varied examples of them.

- *Take defeat well and show good humour.*
- *Do not question officials – accept their decisions.*
- *Say 'well done' to opponents when they do well.*
- *Take other people into consideration when participating in exercise – for example, when swimming avoid colliding with others.*
- *Do not over-celebrate when you do well – take other people's feelings into account and avoid arrogance in victory.*
- *Do not deride the efforts of others – be respectful of others, whatever their ability.*

↑ **Figure 4.1 Etiquette is an important part of sportsmanship.**

## Check your understanding

Tested

1 Which of the following is an example of good sportsmanship when performing a physical activity? *(1 mark)*

   **a)** A football player kicks the ball out of play when he sees an opponent is injured.

   **b)** Obeying the referee in football.

   **c)** Shouting 'well played' to one of your team-mates in hockey.

   **d)** Politely questioning a decision made by the referee in basketball.

2 Give **three** reasons why it is important for all those involved in a physical activity to abide by rules and codes of behaviour. *(3 marks)*

3 Which one of the following is an example of good etiquette when performing a physical activity? *(1 mark)*

   **a)** When the whistle blows in a rugby match you stop playing.

   **b)** Shaking hands with your opponent when you have finished a tennis match.

   **c)** Letting someone win the cycling race because you feel sorry for them.

   **d)** Shouting abuse at the lineswoman in a football match.

# 5. The components of fitness and a healthy, balanced lifestyle

## 5.1 Cardiovascular endurance or stamina                    Revised

The cardiovascular system involves transporting oxygen around the body. The cardiovascular system includes:

- the heart.
- the network of blood vessels.
- the blood that transports essential material around the body.

With a healthy, balanced lifestyle the cardiovascular system can have:

- healthy and more efficient capillaries that allow a greater oxygen uptake.
- a healthy heart that is less likely to suffer from heart disease.
- good blood circulation and an increased amount of blood.

## 5.2 Muscular endurance                    Revised

Muscular endurance is the ability to keep going without rest. /ability of the muscle / group of muscles repeatedly contract / keep going without rest.

With a healthy, balanced lifestyle:

- the muscular system can keep going because of greater aerobic potential. **Activities like swimming or running can enlarge slow-twitch fibres, which gives greater potential for energy production.**
- the heart muscle becomes healthier and after exercise the size of the heart can increase – this is called cardiac hypertrophy.

> **Exam tip**
>
> If examiners ask for the effects of exercise on skeletal muscle then this **excludes** the cardiac muscle (heart).

## 5.3 Speed                    Revised

Speed is the ability of the body to move quickly.

- The movements may be the whole body or parts of the body – **for example, arm speed in cricket bowling in sport.**
- As part of a healthy lifestyle it is often important to be able to move quickly – **for example, when running for a bus.**

With a healthy, balanced lifestyle your speed is affected because:

- your heart and lungs are more efficient.
- your muscles can move quicker because they have more energy available.
- the energy available is greater because your muscles are more efficient in producing energy.

## 5.4 Strength

Revised

Strength is the ability of a muscle to exert force for a short period of time.

The amount of force that can be exerted by a muscle depends on:

- the size of the muscles and the number of muscles involved.
- the coordination of the muscle involved.

As part of a healthy lifestyle it is important to have strength to lift and carry objects and in **sport to be able, for example, to hit a ball harder in tennis.**

With a healthy balanced lifestyle your strength is affected because:

- exercise like cycling can enlarge slow-twitch fibres.
- there are anaerobic benefits to muscle, with activities like sprinting causing the muscle to get bigger and stronger (hypertrophy).

## 5.5 Flexibility

Revised

Flexibility is the amount or range of movement that you can have around a joint.

As part of a healthy lifestyle it is important to have flexibility or suppleness because:

- it enables us to move quicker and more effectively.
- we are less likely to be injured as we go about our daily routines.
- we can reach for objects more effectively.

With a healthy balanced lifestyle your flexibility is affected because:

- our ligaments and supporting tissues can stretch further.
- the more the body is used to stretching, the more able it is to stretch further.

> **Exam tip**
> - Learn and describe the five components of fitness.
> - Be able to give an example why each is important to us both in physical activities and also generally following a healthy lifestyle.

## Check your understanding

Tested

1 Which one of the following describes most accurately cardiovascular endurance? *(1 mark)*

   a) The ability of our body to cope with exercise over a long period of time.

   b) The ability to use muscles over a short period of time.

   c) The amount of force a muscle can exert against a resistance.

   d) The ability to change the body's movement quickly.

2 Which one of the following shows the importance of muscular endurance as a component of a healthy lifestyle? *(1 mark)*

   a) To get jobs done quickly and to have more time for sport.

   b) To be able to reach for things in everyday life without hurting yourself.

   c) To be able to carry your baby brother safely on long walks.

   d) To be determined in all mental and physical activities.

3 Describe why flexibility **and** muscular endurance are important components of fitness and for **each** give a practical example of when they are particularly important in physical activities. *(4 marks)*

OCR GCSE PE    13

**Unit B451 An Introduction to Physical Education**

# 6. The importance of the warm-up and cool-down

## 6.1 The warm-up

- The warm-up should be incorporated in any exercise and training programme and before participating in physical activities.
- The warm-up enables the body to prepare for the onset of exercise.
- It decreases the likelihood of injury and muscle soreness.
- An increase in muscle temperature will help to ensure that there is a ready supply of energy and that the muscle becomes more flexible to prevent injury.
- Improves speed and strength of muscular contraction.

Although it's not explicitly in the specification you will also get credit for knowing that the warm-up causes a release of adrenaline that will start the process of speeding up the delivery of oxygen to the working muscles.

> It gradually raises the body temperature and heart rate and improves gaseous exchange.

↑ **Figure 6.1 It is important to warm up before taking exercise.**

A warm-up might involve the following:

1. Raising the pulse rate by jogging or steady running.
2. Increasing the body or muscle temperature.
3. Stretching the main muscle groups as well as those muscles specifically going to be used by using flexibility or stretching exercises.
4. Stretching for at least 20–30 seconds per main muscle group.
5. Keeping your breathing steady to keep control and to keep calm.
6. Including exercise movements or steady drills that are like the 'real game' situation.
7. Building up the work rate steadily in the warm-up. Start slow and build up work rate ready for the game or competition.
8. Mental preparation for the activity can also be a feature of the warm-up.
9. Mental rehearsal.

## 6.2 The cool-down

- The cool-down is also important for effective training and to follow physical activity.
- A cool-down often consists of light exercising or jogging.

- If light exercise follows training, then the oxygen can more effectively be flushed through the muscle tissue, which oxidises or helps to remove lactic acid.
- It decreases risk of injury or pulling a muscle and decreases risk of muscle soreness or stiffness.

The following points about the cool-down are not stated explicitly in the specification, but you would get credit for them in the exam:

- It also prevents blood pooling in the veins, which can cause dizziness.
- It helps prevent feeling tired or fatigued.
- It *gradually* decreases heart rate and blood pressure.
- It *gradually* decreases body temperature.
- It *gradually* decreases breathing rate.
- It stops you feeling dizzy or faint or sick.
- It has psychological benefits and makes you calm down or lower anxiety.

*gradually returns body to normal temp and working pulse rate to resting pulse rate*

A cool-down might involve the following:

1. Once you have finished any form of physical activity, you should gradually allow your heart rate and breathing to lower to a comfortable level.
2. A good test is to check that you can talk with ease as you exercise.
3. Light aerobic exercise such as walking or easy cycling (sometimes on an exercise bike) is good.
4. Light stretching or a flexibility exercise should also be part of the cool-down, holding each stretch for a minimum of 20–30 seconds, breathing comfortably, with deep breaths through your nose, and out via your mouth.
5. Rehydration is also important, so taking regular sips of water is recommended.

### Exam tip
- A cool-down does not decrease heart rate or breathing or temperature because that would happen anyway if you stop the activity. A cool-down *gradually* allows these decreases.
- Make sure you use a practical example if required by the question.

### Check your understanding                                              Tested

1   Describe an effective warm-up in a physical activity of your choice.                                                                    *(5 marks)*

2   Describe a cool-down for a physical activity. Why is a cool-down important?                                                                 *(5 marks)*

3   Which one of the following is a reason to participate in a warm-up?                                                                    *(1 mark)*

   a) You can stretch out more.

   b) It encourages the crowd to cheer you on.

   c) It increases the tidal volume.

   d) It decreases levels of carbon dioxide.

4   Cooling-down following physical activity is important. Which one of the following is a good reason for performing a cool-down?                                                                    *(1 mark)*

   a) Improves speed of movement.

   b) Raises the pulse rate.

   c) Rehydrates the body.

   d) Prevents muscle soreness.

# 7. The characteristics of skilful movement

- Skilled performers are not born with most motor skills already programmed in their minds – they have to learn them in a number of different ways.

## 7.1 Skill

Revised

There are two main ways of using the word 'skill':

- to see skill as a specific task to be performed.
- to view skill as describing the quality of a particular action.

A movement skill is an action or task that has a goal and that requires voluntary body and/or limb movement to achieve the goal.

Examples of motor skills are:

- a somersault in gymnastics.
- a rugby tackle.
- a tennis serve.
- a football pass.

Examples of skills performed skilfully are:

- a badminton serve that beats the opponent and lands inside the court.
- a hockey pass that finds a fellow player.
- a trampoline routine that is fluent and coordinated.
- a successful scoring shot in football.

Characteristics of skilful movement include the movement being:

- Efficient – **for example, a basketball player will not make unnecessary movements when dribbling the ball up-court.**
- Predetermined: a skilled performer knows what he or she is trying to achieve – **for example, a hockey player knows whereabouts she wants to hit the ball as she shoots at the goal.**
- Coordinated – **for example, a tennis player's movements in the serve are linked together well.**
- Fluent – **for example, a gymnast's floor movements are flowing and coordinated.**
- Aesthetic (looks good when they are performing the skill) – **for example, an athlete performs the high jump with a style that is successful and looks good.**

*eat pretty cakes for Athletes*

Although not directly mentioned in the specification you would also get credit for knowing about the following characteristics of skilful movement:

- Controlled – **for example, a rugby player tackles without using unnecessary movements.**
- Effortless – **for example, a squash player moves around the court without wasting energy.**
- Good technique is shown – **for example, a volleyball player shows the correct technique when blocking the ball at the net.**

● Learned. You do not inherit skills – you learn them by practice and by watching others – **for example, a netball player learns the skill of shooting correctly in PE at school.**

| Unskilled | Skilled |
|---|---|
| Wastes effort | No waste of effort |
| Is slow | Has speed when needed |
| Don't know what they are doing | Knows what they are doing |
| Has jerky (staccato) movements | Is smooth and fluent when moving |
| Looks awkward and uses incorrect technique | Looks good and shows good technique |
| Is rarely successful | Is nearly always successful |

↑ **Table 7.1 Differences between skilled and unskilled participants**

**Exam tip**
● Learn to **describe** these main characteristics of skilled movement and be prepared to give a practical example for each characteristic.
● Be able to describe the differences between unskilled and skilled participants in physical activities.

## Check your understanding
Tested

1 Which one of the following is a good example of the aesthetic characteristic of skilful movement? *(1 mark)*

   a) The rugby player fouls an opponent who tries to run past with the ball.

   b) The movement of the gymnast looks good and is fluent in the floor exercise.

   c) The movement of the volleyball player is fast across the court to get to the ball.

   d) The footballer shouts for the ball because there is no space to shoot.

2 Other than being aesthetic, identify **two** other characteristics of skilful movement, giving a practical example for each. *(4 marks)*

3 Describe **three** characteristics of skilful movement. *(3 marks)*

*Skilled movement = one in which a predetermined objective is accomplished with maximum efficiency and a minimum outlay of energy*

# 8. Performance and outcome goals

Goal setting

- is used to motivate people to exercise and to follow a healthy lifestyle.
- is widely used by sportsmen and women for training and performance.
- can increase confidence.
- helps to control anxiety.

There are two types of goal that can be recognised and set in sport:

- performance goals.
- outcome goals.

## 8.1 Performance goals

Revised

- These are directly related to the performance or technique of the activity – for example, performance goals in netball or football might be to improve passing or shooting techniques.
- Performance goals tend to be short term.

↑ **Figure 8.1 Performance goals in netball might be to improve passing technique.**

Examples of performance goals:

- to improve technique of a front somersault in trampolining.
- to try to stop using a poor golf swing when driving from the tee.
- to improve the running technique in sprinting.
- to shorten the back swing in a tennis serve in order to be more accurate.
- to not let the lifting technique to go wrong when training with heavier weights.

> **Exam tip**
>
> Make sure you know the difference between performance and outcome goals and be able to give practical examples for each.

## 8.2 Outcome goals

- These are concerned with the end result – whether you win or lose – **for example, outcome goals in netball or football might be to win an individual game or a tournament. For instance, a tennis player trying to win the Grand Slam by winning each open tournament has this as their outcome goal.**

- Outcome goals tend to be medium to long term.

Examples of outcome goals:

- to win the 100 metre race in an athletics competition.

- to finish an exercise class without stopping.

- to try to draw level in a cycling race.

- to win the football league.

- to get through to the finals of the golf competition.

### Check your understanding

1 Which one of the following is an example of an outcome goal? *(1 mark)*

   **a)** A tennis player trying to improve his serve.

   **b)** Trying to win a netball match against a local school.

   **c)** A footballer trying to improve her shooting technique.

   **d)** Trying to outwit an opponent when passing the ball in basketball.

2 Which one of the following is an example of a performance goal? *(1 mark)*

   **a)** To win the competition.

   **b)** To improve your technique.

   **c)** To beat your personal best.

   **d)** To please your coach.

3 Describe, using practical examples, performance **and** outcome goal setting when trying to improve performance in a physical activity. *(6 marks)*

# 9. Assessing the body's readiness for exercise

## 9.1 Health Screening

Revised

- Fitness and exercise professionals always advise that before starting a new exercise regime, or if you have any worries over your health, you should get checked out by a General Practitioner (GP).
- The health screening process can include:
  - basic assessment of body composition using Body Mass Index (BMI).
  - cholesterol, blood glucose and iron levels.
  - heart rate.

The following are typical health-screening measurements:

- BMI – This is a measure of body composition. BMI is calculated by taking the person's weight and dividing by their height squared. The higher the BMI, the more body fat is present. However, this is only one indication and other issues such as body type should be taken into consideration. The BMI does not apply to elderly people, pregnant women or highly trained athletes.
- Blood pressure – This is established using a blood pressure-measuring instrument called a sphygmomanometer. Normal blood pressure for men and women is usually considered to be 120/80.
- Resting heart rate – Normal resting heart rates range anywhere from 40 beats per minute up to 100 beats per minute. Ideally, you want to be between 60–90 beats per minute, with the average resting heart rate for a man being 70 beats per minute, and for a woman 75 beats.
- Taking into account family history:
  - A family history of illness or disease can often indicate potential problems. For example, if your parents both suffer with high blood pressure or high levels of cholesterol then you may be at a higher risk of contracting heart disease.

The following health-screening measures are not stated explicitly on the specification but would gain you credit in the exam:

- Cholesterol level – This test should be carried out by a trained nurse or GP. If the level is high then this could increase the likelihood of future illness.
- Glucose level – This test should be carried out by a trained nurse or GP. Unusual amounts of blood glucose might indicate diabetes.

> **Exam tip**
>
> The examiner can only ask about the assessments listed and no others. You are expected to be able to name and describe these assessments or tests and what they actually measure.

## 9.2 Assessing cardio-vascular endurance

Revised

- The level of endurance fitness is indicated by an individual's VO2 max – that is the maximum amount of oxygen an individual can take in and utilise in one minute.
- The potential VO2 max of an individual can be predicted via tests such as:
  - The Cooper's 12-minute walk run test. This involves walking or running around an athletics track as far as possible within 12 minutes.

● The multistage fitness test (sometimes called the 'bleep' or 'beep' test). This test involves a shuttle run that gets progressively more difficult.

## 9.3 Assessing strength
Revised

The strength of an individual can be tested a number of ways:

● One repetition maximum (1 RM) test – this is the maximum weight that can be lifted once with the correct technique. A bench press or leg press are the usual techniques used.
● The grip strength dynamometer is another test for strength – this assesses the strength in the arm muscles by squeezing the hand-grip dynamometer as hard as possible.

## 9.4 Assessing speed
Revised

● This is often tested using the 30-metre or 40-metre sprint (although distances up to 100 metres are suitable).
● The person is timed sprinting the distance as fast as they can.

## 9.5 Assessing flexibility
Revised

● This can be tested via the 'sit and reach test'.
● The objective of this test is to measure the athlete's lower back and hamstring flexibility.
   ● The subject sits on the floor with legs outstretched in a straight position.
   ● The subject reaches as far forward as possible but keeping the legs straight and in contact with the floor.
   ● The distance that the ends of the fingers are from the feet (pointing upwards) is measured.
   ● Using a 'sit and reach' box as shown in Figure 9.1 ensures more accurate measurements. Once again, this test can provide measurements that can be used in assessing any future training and also for the subject to compare performance with national norms.

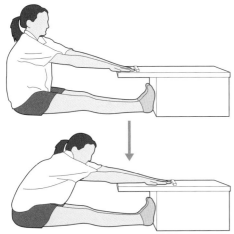

↑ **Figure 9.1 A sit and reach box.**

## 9.6 Validity of tests

Health and safety checks should be done before an assessment or testing session. These should include:

● checking for the proper working of equipment.

● ensuring an adequate supply of safety equipment such as first aid kits.

● giving adequate warm-up when necessary.

● Ensuring that for maximal endurance testing on elderly or others at risk this is done only after medical clearance has been given.

● medical assistance being close at hand, and adequate resuscitation equipment being available nearby.

● ensuring that any person older than 35 years of age, particularly anyone overweight or with a history of high blood pressure and heart disease, consults a medical practitioner before undertaking any vigorous testing.

The testing process involves:

● identification of what is to be measured.

● the selection of a suitable method/test of measuring.

● the collection of data.

● the analysis of the data.

● making decisions about an exercise or fitness programme.

● the implementation of the programme.

In selecting any test it is important to make sure that it is valid and appropriate to the person being tested. All tests should be:

● specific – that is, designed to assess a participant's fitness for the activity/exercise purpose.

● valid – that is, it tests what it is supposed to test.

● reliable – that is, whether the test can be run in the same way again to achieve consistency.

● objective – that is, it produces a consistent result irrespective of the tester.

When you conduct tests, the following points should be taken into consideration:

● Each test should measure one factor only.

● The test should not require any technical competence on the part of the participant – the simpler the better.

● The participant should understand what is required, what is being measured and why it is being measured.

● The test procedure should be strictly standardised to ensure consistency.

Results from testing a participant can be used to:

● create an appropriate training/exercise programme.

● predict future performance/fitness levels.

● indicate weaknesses.

● measure improvement.

● enable you to assess the success of training.

● motivate the person.

The following factors may impede the reliability of your tests: (that is, make them inaccurate):

- the amount of sleep the participant had prior to the test.
- the participant's emotional state/amount of motivation.
- accuracy of measurements (times, distances, etc.).
- temperature, noise and humidity.
- the time of day and caffeine intake.
- other people present – this can improve or impede results.
- the skill of the tester.

## Check your understanding
Tested

1 Which one of the following is a health-screening test?  *(1 mark)*

   a) Sit and reach test

   b) 30-metre sprint test

   c) Blood pressure test ✓

   d) Cooper's 12-minute run test.

2 One way of assessing the body's readiness for exercise is through health screening. Identify **three** other ways of assessing the body's readiness for exercise.  *(3 marks)*

3 Describe how you would use the body mass index (BMI) to assess a young person's readiness for exercise.  *(4 marks)*

# 10. Components of a healthy diet and characteristics of a healthy lifestyle

## 10.1 Essential components of a healthy diet ————— Revised ☐

The following are the main nutrients or essential components that the body requires in order to follow an active, healthy lifestyle.

### Carbohydrates

● Carbohydrates are mainly involved in energy production.

● There are two forms of carbohydrate:

  ● Simple sugars – these provide a quick energy source and include glucose and fructose.

  ● Complex starches – these have many sugar units and are much slower in releasing energy.

● Carbohydrates are very important to those who exercise, especially for exercise that is highly intense.

Examples of carbohydrates are:

● Complex carbohydrates – cereal, pasta, potatoes, bread, fruit.

● Simple carbohydrates – sugar, jam, confectionery, fruit juices.

**Practical consideration: It is recommended that about 60 per cent of an athlete's diet should be made up of carbohydrates.**

↑ **Figure 10.1 Fruit is an important part of a healthy diet.**

### Fats

● These are a major source of energy for performing low-intensity endurance exercise.

● These are either saturated or unsaturated fats.

● Fat consumption should be carefully monitored and can cause obesity. Fat is very important in protecting vital organs and is crucial for cell production and the control of heat loss.

- It is generally accepted that a maximum of 30 per cent of total calories consumed should be from fatty foods.

Examples of sources of fats:

- Saturated fats – meat products, dairy products, cakes, confectionery ← *Harmful*
- Unsaturated fats – oily fish, nuts, margarine, olive oil. ← *Unharmful*

## Protein

- Proteins are known as the building blocks for body tissue and are essential for repair.
- They are also necessary for the production of haemoglobin.
- Protein should account for approximately 15 per cent of total calorie intake.

Examples of sources of protein:

- Meat, fish and poultry are examples of proteins.

## Vitamins

- Vitamins have no calories and are chemical compounds that are needed by the body in small quantities.
- They are vital in the production of energy and prevention of disease and in our metabolism.
- With the exception of vitamin D, the body cannot produce vitamins.
- A well-balanced diet will ensure sufficient vitamin intake.

Examples of sources of vitamins:

- Vitamins can be found in fresh fruit and vegetables.

## Minerals

- These are also empty of calories and are essential for our health.
- There are two types:
  - Macro-minerals, which are needed in large amounts – for example, calcium, potassium and sodium.
  - Trace elements, which are needed in very small amounts – for example, iron, zinc and manganese.
- Minerals can be lost through sweating and so there are implications for those that exercise – minerals should be replaced quickly to ensure good health.

Examples of important minerals are:

- Iron: This is an essential component of haemoglobin, which carries oxygen in the blood. Iron can be found in meat, fish, dairy produce and vegetables. Examples of sources of iron are red meat and offal; watercress.
- Calcium: This mineral is essential for healthy bones and teeth. If there is deficiency in calcium, then there is an increased likelihood of osteoporosis and bone fractures. Calcium is found in milk and dairy products, green vegetables and nuts.

## Water

- This carries nutrients in the body and helps with the removal of waste products.
- It is also very important in the regulation of body temperature.

- The body loses water through urine and sweat. This water loss accelerates depending on the environment and the duration and intensity of any exercise that is being undertaken.

### Fibre

- There are no calories in fibre and it is not digested when we eat it.
- Fibre is only found in the cell walls of plants and is essential to effective bowel function.
- Fibre absorbs a lot of water in the bowel and therefore increases in bulk – this makes the waste softer and more able to be passed out of the body effectively.
- Fibre also decreases the risk of bowel disease and you should intake approximately 18 grams per day.

Examples of sources of fibre:

- Fruit, vegetables and cereal.

## 10.2 Characteristics of a healthy diet  Revised ☐

When planning a diet you should take the following into consideration:

- Food is meant to be enjoyed.
- Avoid too much fat.
- Avoid too many sugary foods.
- Include vitamins and minerals.
- Eat plenty of fibre.
- Keep alcohol within prescribed limits.
- Maintain a balance of intake and output – the intake is the amount of food that the body receives and output is the amount of work the body does or the amount of energy expended.
- Eat plenty of fruit and vegetables. Eating sufficient fruit and vegetables is important for a healthy diet. It helps to reduce the likelihood of coronary heart disease and some cancers.
- If your diet contains too much salt then this may lead to high blood pressure, which can cause heart and kidney disease.

> **Exam tip**
>
> The examiner may ask for a description of a balanced, healthy diet, including hydration and getting a positive energy balance.
>
> Healthy eating involves a daily calorie intake in approximately the following proportions:
> - 50 per cent carbohydrate
> - 30–35 per cent fat
> - 15–20 per cent protein.

## 10.3 Characteristics of a healthy lifestyle  Revised ☐

A balanced, healthy lifestyle will help you to feel better and to live longer. The following are characteristics of a balanced, healthy lifestyle:

- eating a healthy and balanced diet – maintaining a balance of food intake and expenditure of energy.
- **regular exercise – for example, the current government recommendation is that adults should carry out a minimum of 30 minutes' moderate activity on five or more days a week; children and young people aged 5–18 should participate in physical activity of moderate intensity for one hour a day.**
- maintaining a healthy body weight.
- not smoking.
- sensible alcohol consumption.
- maintaining low levels of personal stress.

1 Explain how vitamins **and** minerals contribute to our health. *(4 marks)*

2 Which one of the following is an example of a food high in carbohydrates? *(1 mark)*

   a) Fish

   b) Bananas

   c) Meat

   d) Eggs

3 Which one of the following best indicates a balanced diet? *(1 mark)*

   a) A balance between what is eaten and energy expended.

   b) A balance of different types of protein.

   c) A balance between what is eaten and what is drunk.

   d) A balance between fruit and vegetables.

4 Which one of the following is an essential component of a healthy diet? *(1 mark)*

   a) Pasta

   b) Fish

   c) Water

   d) Bread

5 Describe the characteristics of a balanced diet. *(6 marks)*

6 Which one of the following pairs shows two good examples of characteristics of a balanced, healthy lifestyle? *(1 mark)*

   a) Non-smoking and non-active.

   b) Nutritional diet and regular water drinking.

   c) Non-alcohol and low-protein diet.

   d) Physically active and smoking only a limited number of cigarettes.

# 11. General factors affecting performance and participation

- Our lifestyle affects significantly our fitness and health.
- Many of us now live in a less active way.
- There is an increase in people being overweight and when extreme this is called obesity.
- There are now more instances of diabetes and coronary heart disease, which are affected by the food we eat and our general lifestyle.

Lifestyle factors that can affect our performance and participation in physical activities are listed below.

> **Exam tip**
>
> The examiner may ask you to explain the effects of these factors. Make sure you give reasons in your explanation – remember it is difficult not to explain if you use the word 'because'!

## 11.1 Age                                                        Revised ☐

- Physical activity and sport are often seen as a 'young person's activity' and older people may feel undignified if they participate in sport.
- Discrimination based on age can be shown by others or through lack of access to some activities that are seen as being only for young people.
- Older people may lack self-esteem or confidence to become involved in activity.
- Older people may have poor fitness or health and this can be a barrier to participation.
- Younger participants may also feel discriminated against in some activities or clubs.
- The average life expectancy has increased and so there are more and more older people who could take advantage of physical activity opportunities.
- There are more veterans' teams in a variety of sports and there is a growing awareness that activity in old age can enrich the quality of life experiences.

## 11.2 Gender                                                     Revised ☐

- Certain activities are traditionally linked to either males or females – **for example, boxing is normally associated with men and dance with women.**
- Many men now take up traditionally female activities and many women now take up traditionally male activities – **for example, there are now more men involved in street dance and more women in football.**
- Fewer women take up physical activities than men.
- Some activities discriminate against one particular gender – **for example, golf clubs may only provide smaller time-slots for female participation.**

## 11.3 Disability

Revised

- A lack of suitable facilities or access such as no wheelchair ramps or doors that are too narrow can prevent participation in activities.
- Those with disabilities may not be able-bodied enough to participate in some activities.
- A lack of self-esteem or lack of self-confidence can also affect participation.
- Discrimination from others may dissuade those that are disabled from participating.
- However, those with disabilities can now have much better access to physical activities.
- Disability sport is recognised as a sport in its own right, with UK participants who have achieved great success in international competitions.

## 11.4 Alcohol consumption

Revised

- This is a concentrated source of energy but one that is not available during exercise for our working muscles.
- Therefore many performers in sport or those who wish to be active and healthy do not drink alcohol and most drink very little.
- The Health Development Agency recommends for adults, if they must drink alcohol:
  - Males – 3–4 units per day.
  - Females – 2–3 units per day.
- 'Binge drinking' is particularly bad for you, and this is a growing habit amongst teenagers and young adults.
- It is better to spread your alcohol consumption across the week and to leave some alcohol-free days.
- One unit
  - 1/2 pint 'ordinary strength' beer = 3.0–3.5 % alcohol = 90 calories.
  - 1 standard glass of wine = 11% alcohol = 90 calories.
  - single measure spirits = 38% alcohol = 50 calories.

## 11.5 Smoking

Revised

- There is overwhelming evidence that health and fitness are affected adversely by smoking, whatever age you are.
- Cigarettes contain tar, nicotine, carbon monoxide and other irritants that cause disease.
- Normally haemoglobin in the blood carries oxygen but when carbon monoxide is in the blood, then haemoglobin prefers to carry this and therefore carries less oxygen.
- The time taken to complete activities that are physical is increased after smoking.
- Endurance and capacity for exercise are reduced by smoking.
- Training has less effect on smokers.

*Unit B451 An Introduction to Physical Education*

- Smoking is the biggest cause of preventable death in the Western world. It kills more than 120,000 in the UK every year, with most dying from three main diseases: cancer, chronic obstructive lung disease (bronchitis and emphysema) and coronary heart disease.

## 11.6 Over-eating and under-eating
Revised

- A balanced diet is important for a healthy lifestyle.
- The amount that is eaten must be balanced with how much activity you undertake.

The effects of over-eating are that:

- you carry too much weight to be able to participate in physical activities and this may lead to lack of mobility.
- you lack agility, speed and coordination.
- you may suffer from poor health or develop diseases such as Type 2 diabetes.
- you feel tired and lethargic.
- you may lack motivation.
- you may feel embarrassment and have low self-esteem.
- other people may discriminate against or bully you.
- You are less flexible.
- Over-eating can put too much strain on the heart.
- You could be obese.
- You feel sick or ill and possibly experience stomach cramps.

The effects of under-eating are:

- you have a lack of energy and get tired easily.
- you may suffer from muscle wastage.
- you are more likely to be ill.
- you are unlikely to receive the right nutrients or vitamins.
- you lack strength.
- you may feel embarrassed and have low self-esteem.
- others might discriminate against or bully you.

## 11.7 Performance-enhancing drugs
Revised

- The use of performance-enhancing drugs (for example, anabolic steroids) is widespread and can seriously affect health and well-being.
- Addiction to such drugs causes anxiety, depression and lowering of self-esteem.
- Performance drugs contravene the ethics of sport and undermine the principles of fair participation.
- Some drug misuse may cause serious side effects, which can compromise an athlete's health.
- Using substances to mask pain or injury could make an injury worse or cause permanent damage.
- Illegality – it is forbidden by law to possess or supply some substances.

## Blood doping

- This involves the administration of products that enhance the uptake, transport and delivery of oxygen.
- Blood is removed and the body replaces this. Then the blood is re-infused into the body, which increases the blood volume and the amount of haemoglobin.

Problems associated with blood doping include:

- infections from the injection site or blood infections and the risk of AIDS.
- an increase in blood pressure and an increase in blood viscosity.
- heart problems.
- kidney failure.
- having psychological problems and a sense of guilt.
- being banned from the sport or fined.
- bringing your activity into disrepute and letting other people down.

## Anabolic steroids

- These are man-made drugs that increase muscle growth if taken with vigorous training.
- This also enables the athlete to recover quicker and therefore to be able to train even harder.

The main problems with taking such drugs are:

- both the liver and kidneys can develop tumours.
- high blood pressure.
- severe acne or spots.
- shrinking of the testicles and reduced sperm count and the development of breasts in males.
- the growth of facial hair, baldness and deepening of the voice in females.
- an increase in aggression and other psychological problems.

## Check your understanding                                              Tested

1 Explain the effects of under-eating on performance **and** participation in physical activity.                         (4 marks)

2 Which one of the following shows the effects of gender on participation in a physical activity?                        (1 mark)

   a) Females have lower levels of concentration than males in physical activities.

   b) Males feel more pain than females in physical activities.

   c) Males are less likely to participate in traditionally female activities.

   d) Females are less likely to show high skill levels in physical activities.

3 Performance-enhancing drugs are used by some performers to try and gain an advantage over their opponents. Describe the effects of performance-enhancing drugs on the performer.                         (4 marks)

4 Give **four** ways that disability might affect participation in physical activities.                                   (4 marks)

# 12. Indicators of health and well-being

The following measurements called 'indicators' give us a picture of how well we are doing and also give an overall view of what we should be aiming for.

- Satisfaction with aspects of life.
  - How satisfied we feel about our lives overall.
  - This does not mean that you will feel deliriously happy about everything but overall to be healthy and a balanced individual you need to be pretty satisfied with the way things are generally going.
- Frequency of positive and negative feelings.
  - This means how often you feel very positive about life around you and how often you have negative thoughts.
  - The more positive thoughts that you have, the more healthy and balanced you are likely to be both mentally and physically.
- Frequency of feelings or activities that may have a positive or negative impact on well-being.
  - Some of the feelings that you have or activities that you are involved in may have a real impact on how you feel, others often do not – **for example, if you regularly play sport you may feel excited and enjoy being with others**. This has a positive impact on the way you feel.

↑ **Figure 12.1 Those who are active in many different ways are often the happiest.**

  - If you are taking illegal drugs or are consuming too much alcohol, this may also make you feel good in the short term but may have a lasting negative impact on your health and well-being.
- Access to green space.
  - Do you have places around you that give you a sense of space?
  - Those who live in overcrowded conditions and do not have anywhere around them that is spacious and has vegetation may well feel less good, which may have an impact on their health and well-being.

> **Exam tip**
>
> The examiner may ask for a description of these measures and indicators and ask for practical examples – for example, being satisfied with life may include having a balance of healthy activities and having a good work–life balance.

- Level of participation in other activities.
  - Those who are active in many different ways are often the happiest.
  - Usually if you have a variety of interests then you have a better view of yourself and others.
- Positive mental health
  - If you feel happy or optimistic about the future and feel useful, then you are more likely to have positive mental health.
  - Those who are more relaxed, feel interested in other people and deal with problems well also are said to have positive mental health.

## Check your understanding

Tested

1 One of the measures or indicators of health and well-being is access to green space – in other words, open spaces for exercise. Identify **three** other measures or indicators of health and well-being. *(3 marks)*

2 Positive mental health can be an indicator of health and well-being. Which one of the following shows positive mental health? *(1 mark)*

a) Staying out of trouble

b) Regular eating

c) Feeling happy

d) Regular fitness training.

3 Which one of the following is **not** a good indicator of health and well-being? *(1 mark)*

a) Participating regularly in physical activities

b) High level of income

c) Satisfaction with life

d) Feeling positive about life.

4 Give reasons why access to green space is a good indicator of your physical and mental well-being. *(4 marks)*

# 13. Methods of exercise and training

## 13.1 Circuit training
Revised

- This involves a series of exercises that are arranged in a particular way called a circuit because the training involves repetition of each activity.
- The resistance (what we have to work against) that is used in circuits relates mainly to body weight and each exercise in the circuit is designed to work on a particular muscle group.
- For effective training different muscle groups should be worked on, with no two of the same muscle groups being worked on one after the other – **for example, an activity that uses the main muscle groups in the arms should then be followed, for example, by an exercise involving the muscle groups in the legs.**
- Typical types of exercises that are involved in circuit training are press-ups, star jumps, dips and squat thrusts.
- Circuit training can also incorporate skills in the activities – **for example, hockey players may include dribbling activities, flicking the ball, shuttle runs and shooting activities.**
- The duration and intensity depends on the type of activities that have been used. **An example would be a circuit with 1 minute's worth of activity, followed by 1 minute's worth of rest. The whole circuit could then be repeated three times. Scores at the end of the circuit may be related to time or repetitions and are a good way of motivating in training.**

### Exam tip
The examiner will ask for a description of the following methods and a brief description of how each helps in health and fitness.

## 13.2 Aerobics including body pump, spin and dance exercise
Revised

- These are all a type of cardiovascular exercise and involve any sustained, rhythmic activity that uses large muscle groups.
- Aerobic exercise also makes the lungs work harder as the body's need for oxygen is increased.
- The local gym will provide a wide variety of aerobic options, such as treadmills, cross trainers, exercise bikes, stairmasters, rowing and ski machines.
- Many gyms and leisure centres provide classes, such as various forms of dance, body pump, body combat and step aerobics with a trained instructor.
- Always check that the instructor is suitably qualified.
- Body pump is exercising with weights to music together with others in an exercise class.
- Spin is an exercise class that uses static bikes or ergometers.
- Dance exercise involves dance movements to music, with vigorous sequences that often last at least 20 minutes.

## 13.3 Aqua aerobics

Revised

- This is aerobic exercise in the water.
- It takes place normally in shallow water at a swimming pool and as part of an organised group session that can last anywhere between 30 minutes and an hour.
- Workouts usually comprise routines familiar to those who have experienced land aerobics, and could include jumping jacks, cross-country skiing motion and walking and running backwards and forwards.
- The support that the water provides for the body greatly reduces the risk of bone, muscle and joint injury, its density meaning that 90 per cent of a body's weight is supported.
- Aqua aerobics is a good activity for those wanting to improve the health of their heart and lungs and burn some calories without too much risk of injury.

## 13.4 Yoga

Revised

- Yoga, was developed by the ancient wise men of India and is a system of personal development involving body, mind and spirit that dates back more than 5000 years.
- The aim of this approach of both mind and body control is physical health and happiness, together with mental peace and tranquillity.
- Yoga helps to develop strength and flexibility.

↑ **Figure 13.1 Yoga is good for general fitness.**

## 13.5 Pilates

Revised

- Pilates is an exercise method developed by its founder Joseph Pilates to try to improve physical and mental health.
- Pilates focuses on building your body's **core strength** and improving your posture through a series of low repetition, low impact stretching and conditioning exercises.

## Check your understanding

Tested

1 Which one of the following would be a good method of exercise to improve your stamina? *(1 mark)*

   **a)** Yoga

   **b)** Pilates

   **c)** Sprinting

   **d)** Aerobics

2 Which one of the following pairs of fitness components is yoga likely to develop? *(1 mark)*

   **a)** Flexibility and cardiovascular endurance

   **b)** Speed and flexibility

   **c)** Strength and flexibility

   **d)** Muscular endurance and cardiovascular endurance

# 14. Levels of participation

Make sure you:

1 understand and can apply patterns and trends of participation in different age groups.

2 know approximately the numbers of people participating regularly in sporting activity at the recommended level.

● Participation rates. This refers to the number of people within a group who are involved in sport compared with those who are not – **for example, in a school the participation rates of girls in extra-curricular sport could be 30 per cent.**

The following are generally recognised as being groups of people who are not getting a fair chance in sport:

● ethnic minority communities.
● people with disabilities.
● women.
● the 50+ age group.

**Exam tip**

The specification states that you should know the participation trends and be able to explain some of the reasons for participation or non-participation.

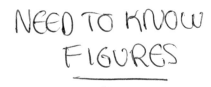

NEED TO KNOW FIGURES

## 14.1 Patterns and trends for different age groups

Revised ☐

● In a variety of studies it has been shown that about three-quarters of adults had taken part in some sport, game or physical activity within twelve months.

● In general, participation rates decrease with age.

● The proportion of adults who take part in at least one sport or physical activity generally decreases with age.

● 77 per cent of 16 to 19 year olds take part in at least one physical activity (including walking).

● 30 per cent of people aged 70 and over take part in at least one physical activity (including walking).

● Walking is the most popular activity for all age groups.

● Participation in many activities is very strongly related to age.

● Participation in golf is maintained at a fairly similar level up to age 69, with the average age of participants being about 42.

● Participation rates in swimming and keep fit/yoga remain at similar levels between the ages of 16 and 44, after which they fall.

● Participants in bowls peak among 60 to 69 year olds.

## 14.2 Numbers of people participating regularly in physical activities at the recommended level

Revised ☐

● The recommended amount of exercise is one hour every day for children and 30 minutes at least five times a week for adults. Recent indications are that two-thirds were failing to hit the target, with a fifth saying they only exercised once a month or less.

- In terms of participation the five most popular sports, games or physical activities among adults in the UK are approximately:
  - walking (46 per cent).
  - swimming (35 per cent).
  - keep fit/yoga – including aerobics and dance exercise (22 per cent).
  - cycling (19 per cent).
  - cue sports: billiards, snooker and pool (17 per cent).
- Men are more likely than women to participate in sports activities – about 51 per cent of men compared with 36 per cent of women.
- The most popular activities are walking and swimming.
- 44 per cent of men and 31 per cent of women who participate in at least one activity (excluding walking and darts) belong to a sports club.
- Overall, men were more likely than women to have participated in an organised competition, with about 40 per cent of men competing, compared with 14 per cent of women.

## Check your understanding

Tested

1 Which one of the following age groups participates most in physical activities? *(1 mark)*

   a) 16–24 years of age

   b) 25–34 years of age

   c) 35–44 years of age

   d) 45–59 years of age

2 Which one of the following is the correct proportion of adults who take part in physical activity? *(1 mark)*

   a) 80 per cent of 70 year olds

   b) 50 per cent of 70 year olds

   c) 70 per cent of 18 year olds

   d) 20 per cent of 18 year olds

3 Which one of the following is the most popular in terms of participation in the UK for all age groups? *(1 mark)*

   a) Football

   b) Walking

   c) Pilates

   d) Badminton

4 Describe the trends of participation in physical activities. *(4 marks)*

# 15. Reasons for participation

- There is a difference in the participation levels between men and women in physical activities and sport. There are far more men than women getting involved in sport, either participating or spectating.

- It is still thought by some people that being good at sport or interested in sport is unfeminine, thus reinforcing male dominance in sport and sport coverage.

- Of course, there are many positive aspects of female physical activities and sport. More women are now involved in physical exercise and there is far more interest in health and fitness matters.

The following are some of the main reasons why people often participate in physical activity:

- Health reasons.
- To manage stress.
- To feel good.
- To have a good sense of well-being.
- To live longer.
- To improve or maintain an image.
- For enjoyment.
- To meet people and make friends.
- As a hobby – something to do.
- To please or to copy parents or role models.
- To make money or as a job.

> **Exam tip**
>
> Examination questions are likely to ask for an explanation of *why* people participate in physical activities – so state the reason and then explain by giving more information or a practical example. For example, 'Some people participate to make friends – for example, join an exercise class to meet new people'.

↑ **Figure 15.1 Participating in sport can help us make friends and socialise.**

Benefits to those who participate:

- Benefits to our health and fitness – physical activity and sport can make us fitter and therefore healthier.

- Benefits to our well-being. Many people report that they feel better after participating in physical activity or sport.

- Benefits to combat stress. Many people often use physical activity and sport as an escape from their working life.

- There are benefits to learning new skills, for example, gaining a sense of accomplishment, being able to compete eventually at a higher level and increasing our self-satisfaction when we overcome challenges and barriers.

- The benefit of socialising and participating with other people. New friends can be made through physical activity and sport and this is important again for our sense of well-being.

## Check your understanding

1 Many people participate in physical activities and follow an active, healthy lifestyle. Which one of the following is a **health** reason for **regular participation** in physical activities? *(1 mark)*

   a) To make friends.

   b) To have a job and earn money.

   c) To be a good role model.

   d) To manage stress more effectively.

2 Give **three** reasons why a performer might participate in physical activities. *(3 marks)*

3 Which one of the following is a reason that is social for participating in physical activities? *(1 mark)*

   a) To join a climbing club to make friends.

   b) To try to reach your personal best in a gymnastics competition.

   c) To enjoy winning in a football match.

   d) To regularly jog after work.

# 16. Reasons for non-participation

- People of all ages are not participating in physical activity nor are they following an active, healthy lifestyle.

- More and more people are now obese.

- There is an increase in diseases linked to poor lifestyle such as diabetes Type 2 and some cancers and, of course, cardiovascular disease.

The main reasons for not participating are:

- Health reasons – **for example, an older man may suffer from arthritis so finds it difficult to participate in exercise classes.**

- Disability – **for example, a disabled person may not be able to participate in swimming because of the lack of support equipment.**

- Injury – **for example, a 16-year-old girl cannot continue with her aerobics class because she has twisted her ankle.**

- Discrimination – **for example, a middle-aged woman is not allowed to join a golf club because it is a male-only club.**

- Peer pressure – **for example, your friends don't want you to play basketball because they want you to go out clubbing instead.**

- Cultural – **for example, a teenage girl is not allowed to go swimming with her friends because wearing a bathing costume in public is not allowed in her culture.**

- Lack of time and other pressures – **for example, a middle-aged man thinks that he has no time to exercise because he has too much work to do at the office.**

- Too much technology: There is less need to walk so much nowadays and leisure is often more passive. **For example, a young boy does not see the point of going out on his bicycle when he could be at home watching television or playing on his PlayStation.**

- Lack of confidence and self esteem – **for example, a teenage boy may not want to join a street dance class because he lacks confidence in his dancing ability.**

- Lack of positive influences from others such as parents and other role models – **for example, a young girl's parents do not see the point of sport and think it's 'unladylike'.**

- Lack of opportunities and access to facilities as well as money – **for example, a teenager does not join any activity clubs because there is nowhere close by and money is tight because the parents are out of work.**

> **Exam tip**
>
> The examiner may ask you to give a reason or to give reasons with practical examples. So for each of the reasons identified make sure that you can write a practical example that shows why some people do not participate in physical activities.

1 Discrimination is one reason why some people do not participate in physical activities. Which of the following is an example of discrimination? *(1 mark)*

   a) Boys not selecting dance as one of their physical activities for assessment.

   b) Disabled pupils not choosing to participate in a physical exercise session.

   c) Women not being allowed to play golf at peak times at their golf club.

   d) Elderly people going for a swim at their local swimming pool.

2 Describe why young people may give up participating in physical activities when they leave school. *(6 marks)*

3 Which one of the following is an example of peer pressure that prevents participation in physical activities? *(1 mark)*

   a) Watching your local rugby team rather than playing.

   b) Friends telling you that physical activity is for 'losers'.

   c) Giving up sport because of your part-time job.

   d) Preferring to play computer games.

# 17. Specific social, cultural and locational reasons affecting participation

- Age – You, or others, think you are too young or too old for an activity.
- Gender – Certain activities are traditionally linked to either males or females and this can lead to discrimination.
- Education – Those who have had more opportunities in their school may participate more.
- Family – People who have members of their family who value sport and physical activity are more likely to participate. If your family generally does not think that it is worth being active then you are less likely to participate in physical activities.
- Disability – If you have a disability you may be discriminated against.

↑ **Figure 17.1 Disability discrimination is one reason for non-participation.**

- Access to facilities – This may be difficult or you may yourself feel that you are unable to participate.
- Ethnicity – Some ethnic groups may support physical activity while others may not.
- Religion – As above, some people may perceive that their religion does not support participation or certain types of participation. Others may support and encourage it.
- Environment – If you live in an area that has good outdoor facilities, for example, then you may be more likely to get involved in outdoor adventurous activities.
- Climate – This often dictates whether the activity can be indoors or outdoors.

The following factors affecting participation in sport are not mentioned on the specification, however they are all valid and would gain you credit in the exam:

- Cultural barriers – Our culture in the UK is diverse and multicultural but in physical activity and sport there are still examples and practices that show discrimination. **For example, if a boy wants to be involved** in ballet or a girl wants to play rugby, there are many social pressures to obstruct their participation.

- **Funding barriers** can also exist, with many sports seemingly out of reach for many people because they cannot afford the equipment, facilities or membership fees to participate.
- It may also be very difficult for people to afford the time away from work and family commitments to be involved in sport.
- Time – **For example, many people decide not to participate in physical activity because of work commitments.**
- Resources – Depending on where you live, you may or may not have facilities or sports clubs near to you.
- Fitness/ability – Some people do not join in with physical activities because they think that they are not good enough. This perception may well have arisen from previous experiences, for example, at school.
- Peer pressure – If a group that a young person belongs to does not value participation in physical activity then it would be very difficult for that young person to be involved in such activity.
- Health problems – There are genuine health reasons for some people not to participate in physical activity, although many medical practitioners will encourage an active lifestyle as much as possible.
- Access – Although there are more low-cost courses available nowadays, there is still the problem of being able to afford to participate in physical activities.

## Check your understanding
Tested

1  Identify the positive and negative effects of the family on participation in physical activities. *(4 marks)*

2  Which one of the following shows that ethnicity can affect participation in physical activity? *(1 mark)*
   a) If you are tall then you will be able to jump higher.
   b) You are more likely to be involved in physical activity if your friends are involved.
   c) You may not be selected for a team because of the colour of your skin.
   d) Northern European people are better at swimming.

3  Which one of the following is an example of climate affecting levels of participation in the UK? *(1 mark)*
   a) Very few boys get involved in ballet in the UK.
   b) Very few people get involved in skiing in the UK.
   c) No swimming pool available in the area.
   d) Many girls play netball in school.

# 18. School Key Processes and influences on participation

- Physical Education lessons – These encourage the development of skills, used in many physical activities and sports.
- Extra-curricular sports activities that are organised can involve teams and clubs for a range of physical activities.
- Examination courses in Physical Education have raised the awareness of the role of sport in society and the need for a healthy lifestyle.
- Links between schools and local sports clubs and other recreation providers enable more opportunities for participation for young people.
- The National Curriculum is a government list of courses that must be delivered in all state schools from primary schools to the age of 16 in secondary schools.
- One of the stated aims of the National Curriculum is to get as many children to actively participate in physical activities and sport via Key Processes.

## 18.1 Key Processes and how they influence participation

Revised

The following are the essential skills and processes in the PE curriculum that pupils need to learn in order to make progress.

- Key Process 1: Developing skills in physical activity. Pupils should be able to:
  - refine and adapt skills into techniques.
  - develop the range of skills they use.
  - develop the precision, control and fluency of their skills.
- Key Process 2: Making and applying decisions. Pupils should be able to:
  - select and use tactics, strategies and compositional ideas effectively in different creative, competitive and challenge type contexts.
  - refine and adapt ideas and plans in response to changing circumstances.
  - plan and implement what needs practising to be more effective in performance.
  - recognise hazards and make decisions about how to control any risks to themselves and others.
- Key Process 3: Developing physical and mental capacity. Pupils should be able to:
  - develop their physical strength, stamina, speed and flexibility to cope with the demands of different activities.
  - develop their mental determination to succeed.
- Key Process 4: Evaluating and improving. Pupils should be able to:
  - analyse performances, identifying strengths and weaknesses.

- make decisions about what to do to improve their performance and the performance of others.
- act on these decisions in future performances.
- be clear about what they want to achieve in their own work and what they have actually achieved.
- Key Process 5: Making informed choices about healthy, active lifestyles. Pupils should be able to:
  - identify the types of activity they are best suited to.
  - identify the types of role they would like to take on.
  - make choices about their involvement in healthy physical activity.

**Exam tip**

For each of the Key Processes make sure that you can give a practical example of this taking place in school.

## 18.2 Practical examples for each Key Process

Revised

- Developing skills – **for example, teaching hockey skills.**
- Making and applying decisions – **for example, a pupil umpiring a netball match in a PE lesson.**
- Developing physical and mental capacity – **for example, a pupil as leader running a Year 8 football session.**
- Evaluating and improving – **for example, a fellow pupil assessing your performance in gymnastics.**
- Making informed decisions about lifestyle – **for example, in a GCSE theory session being taught about healthy eating.**

## Check your understanding

Tested

1 Describe how you would evaluate **and** help to improve someone's performance in a physical activity. *(6 marks)*

2 Which one of the following is a Key Process in physical education? *(1 mark)*

  a) Effort

  b) Competence

  c) Developing skills and techniques

  d) Performance.

3 Which one of the following is a good example of decision making when participating in physical activities? *(1 mark)*

  a) Choosing a local team to support even though they have a low league position.

  b) Choosing to follow a GCSE course in physical education.

  c) Choosing the right diet to lose weight.

  d) Choosing the right pass to one of your team-mates.

4 Which one of the following is **not** a role of the school curriculum in promoting an active, healthy lifestyle? *(1 mark)*

  a) Teaching motor skills.

  b) Developing leadership roles.

  c) Encouraging participation in activities.

  d) Selecting the best performers for national teams.

# 19. Pathways for involvement in physical activity

- **Pathway 1** – Regularly and actively getting involved in Physical Education, sport, dance and healthy activity.

  - **For example, regular attendance at PE classes with very few instances of not being able to participate.**

  - **For example, being involved in extra-curricular clubs or sports teams in your school or college.**

  - **For example, involvement in dance activities as well as exercise or fitness classes.**

- **Pathway 2** – Taking part in school and community sport and dance opportunities.

  - This involves you taking up the opportunities that are available either in your school or college or in the local community.

  - Your school may run a number of different activities, clubs and classes as a pathway to being involved but you have the choice whether you wish to be involved.

  - Your local community may well run classes as part of a night school provision – **For example, sports such as five-a-side football or netball or keep fit classes, such as body pump or dance exercise.**

> **Exam tip**
>
> You should be able to describe each pathway and have a practical example for each.

↑ **Figure 19.1 A pathway to getting involved in physical activity could be to participate in community activity classes.**

- **Pathway 3** – To become a performer, leader or official and working towards qualification.

  - Coaching badges and awards for participation (for example, in swimming) are often available as ways in which you can be involved in physical activities.

  - These qualifications often motivate people to want to be involved in physical activities.

- **Pathway 4** – Being involved in increasingly complex and challenging tasks and activities.
  - When you are involved in physical activities you may wish to go further as you get more experienced.
  - This pathways involves you pushing yourself and taking up personal challenges.
  - This can be a very motivating and rewarding pathway.
- **Pathway 5** – Reaching the highest possible standards of involvement in physical activity.
  - This pathway is about trying to reach your potential in physical activity.
  - Whatever the role you chose – whether as a participant, a leader or an official – you can strive to be better at what you do and raise your own personal standards.
  - This pathway will potentially give you a great sense of achievement.
- **Pathway 6** – Pursuing routes into sport through volunteering.
  - This pathway involves some research into what might be available to you as a volunteer.
  - There are many routes and roles you can play especially in helping to organise and lead activities.
  - You may wish to volunteer and help within your school – perhaps with lower school activities or within your local community.
  - You may, for example, wish to help in a local care home for the elderly assisting in running activities that encourage more activity for elderly residents.
  - You might volunteer, for example, in national and international competitions such as the Olympic Games.

## Check your understanding

Tested

1. Which one of the following is **not** a pathway for involvement in physical activities? *(1 mark)*

   a) Regularly taking part in physical education.

   b) Becoming an umpire in hockey.

   c) Volunteering to help organise the 2012 Olympic Games.

   d) To regularly watch your favourite football team.

2. Describe the possible pathways of involvement in physical activities. *(6 marks)*

3. There are many pathways we can choose to be involved in physical activities. Which one of the following describes community sport as a pathway for involvement in physical activity? *(1 mark)*

   a) Representing your school hockey team.

   b) Playing your best to win for your school team.

   c) Helping to coach hockey at your local club.

   d) Watching the local hockey team at a home game.

# 20. Learning skills

We learn skills related to sport in three basic ways:

● By making associations or links between what we see and hear (stimuli) and what we can do (response) by practising or rehearsing actions.

● By observing others and then copying them.

● By using experiences of trial and error.

## 20.1 Practice and rehearsal

Revised

● We often practise repetitive skills drills that encourage movements to become almost automatic – **For example, a hockey player dribbling the ball recognises a route opening to the goal and runs into that opening to take a shot at the goal in an almost automatic response. This response has been practised many times in training when the stimulus of the opening becomes apparent.**

● The responses of the learner will become conditioned when associated with a particular stimulus.

● A possible problem with the 'drill' style of teaching motor skills is that the participant cannot gain an understanding of why he or she is doing something.

↑ **Figure 20.1**

## 20.2 Trial and error learning of motor skills

Revised

● Trial and error learning, sometimes called operant conditioning, involves the shaping of our movements and techniques through the use of reinforcement.

● Trial and error learning is widely used in the teaching of motor skills and is extremely effective. Rewards are used extensively in skills teaching because they reinforce the type of movements or techniques required. **For example, if you wished to teach a deep serve in tennis, you might draw a large chalk circle at the back of the opposing service box and ask the learner to try to serve into the chalk circle. After numerous practice sessions, which would be increasingly successful, you would draw a smaller circle and encourage the learner to serve into the smaller target.**

**Exam tip**

Be prepared to describe each method of learning skills and explain how each works by using a practical example – **for example, a netball player will try out different methods of passing to see which one works best: this is called trial and error learning.**

## 20.3 Copying others – observational learning

- This involves the influences of other people. Learning takes place through the observation and copying or imitation of others.

- The person whose behaviour or skills and techniques are being observed is called the role model.

- We are more likely to copy those who show what we think is acceptable behaviour or skills and techniques.

- Top sports people sometimes forget that they are enthusiastically watched by many young viewers who will try to copy their every move – they are role models, whose behaviour is seen as acceptable and preferable to that of others.

- When teaching skills, it is the demonstration process that is particularly important in observational learning. **For example, if a coach or teacher of gymnastics wanted to demonstrate the handstand or use another performer to demonstrate, it is best if:**

  - the demonstrator is **successful** and is **good** at the activity.

  - aspects of the demonstration are **highlighted**, such as the position of the arms.

  - the demonstration is **repeated.**

  - the activity is then **practised and rehearsed.**

  - there are **rewards** available, such as praise to **encourage** copying.

### Check your understanding

Tested

1 Which one of the following is the most appropriate role model for learning physical activity skills? *(1 mark)*

   **a)** A well-qualified coach.

   **b)** A friend who is also learning new skills.

   **c)** A successful sports team that you watch.

   **d)** A top quality newspaper.

2 Physical activity skills can be learned by using a variety of methods. Describe, using practical examples, methods that assist in the learning of physical activity skills. *(6 marks)*

3 Which one of the following is the **least** effective way to learn physical activity skills? *(1 mark)*

   **a)** Trial and error

   **b)** Copy role models

   **c)** Practise hard

   **d)** Reading a coaching manual.

4 Which one of the following is an example of trial and error when learning movement skills? *(1 mark)*

   **a)** Watching a video of basketball shooting technique.

   **b)** Copying your coach's demonstration of the forehand drive technique in tennis.

   **c)** Practising shooting in hockey to get the right technique.

   **d)** Listening to your teacher's instructions about the handstand technique in gymnastics.

# 21. Feedback and motivation

## 21.1 Feedback

Revised ✓

- Feedback can be given during the performance of a motor skill or after its completion.
- Feedback is most effective if it is given close to the performance so the performance is fresh in the participant's mind.
- Feedback motivates, changes performance or actually reinforces learning.

There are several forms of feedback:

- Knowledge of results
  - This feedback is external and can come from the performer seeing the result of their response or from another person, usually a coach or teacher.
- Knowledge of performance
  - This is feedback about the pattern of movement that has taken, or is taking, place.

Both knowledge of results and knowledge of performance can help with the motivation of a performer, but if used incorrectly they can also demotivate.

- Internal/intrinsic feedback – this is a type of continuous feedback that comes from within yourself.
- External/extrinsic/augmented feedback – feedback that comes from external sources, for example, from sound or vision.

A and A* students might also wish to remember the following, for extra marks:

- Continuous feedback – feedback during the performance, either from the coach, instructor or teacher or from the continuous feel of the skill.
- Terminal feedback – feedback after the response has been completed.
- Positive feedback – reinforces skill learning and gives information about a successful outcome.
- Negative feedback – information about an unsuccessful outcome or getting things wrong.
  - Negative feedback can be used effectively at times as a motivational tool.

> **Exam tip**
>
> You should be able to show how feedback can encourage and motivate participants to follow an active, healthy lifestyle.

## 21.2 Motivation

Revised

### Motivation in the role of participant

- Intrinsic motivation is the internal drive or willpower that people have to participate in physical activities or to perform well in sport.
  - Intrinsic motives include fun, enjoyment and the satisfaction that is experienced by achieving something or simply by doing it for its

own sake. **For example, a club tennis player who is 50 years of age reports that when he plays he often feels a sense of relief from the day's stresses and strains and that he enjoys the hard physical work of playing tennis.**

- Extrinsic motivation involves influences external to the performer. For instance, the drive to do well in physical activity or sport could come from the need to please others or to gain rewards like medals or badges, or in some cases from large amounts of money.

  - Extrinsic motivation can increase levels of intrinsic motivation. **If, for example, you win the cup in boxing this will probably result in you feeling good about the activity and enjoying boxing in future bouts. If you get praise from your family for exercising after school you will feel good when exercising.**

## Motivation for the roles of leader and official

- The role of leader – **You may want to take on a leadership role, for example, to run a lower school football or netball team. Whatever your leadership role you may lead because you enjoy the feeling of encouraging others (intrinsic) or you may like the praise from others and the recognition that you are doing a good job (extrinsic).**

- The role of official – **You might wish to umpire or referee a game for others or you may volunteer to be a basketball table official. You might like the power it gives you and that it makes you feel good – this is intrinsic motivation. You may be striving to achieve a coaching qualification to further your career –this is extrinsic motivation.**

## Check your understanding
Tested ☐

1  Which one of the following is the best example of how knowledge of results can motivate a young person?  *(1 mark)*

   a) To show a young person that they have run a distance quicker than they have before.

   b) To show a video playback of a javelin throw to an athlete.

   c) To give a badge for a gymnast who learns a new skill.

   d) To give money to a young person who stops smoking.

2  Which one of the following is the best example of intrinsic feedback?  *(1 mark)*

   a) A demonstration of a skill to be learned.

   b) The feeling that a participant gets when they have performed well.

   c) First aid is available if needed.

   d) The teacher says 'Well done' if the skill is performed correctly.

3  Explain, using practical examples, how you might motivate a young person to be involved as an **official** in a physical activity.  *(6 marks)*

# 22. Goal setting

By setting goals you can:

● Take up an activity or activities and stick to an exercise programme (exercise adherence) – **for example, a young mother sets a goal of exercising once a week and sticks to her exercise programme.**

● Control your anxiety or levels of stress – **for example, a dancer sets a goal of performing a short routine in front of a large audience. When she achieves this it lowers her levels of anxiety.**

● Improve your performance (optimise performance) – **for example, a football player sets a goal of improving his shooting technique and this leads to more goals being scored.**

Although not mentioned explicitly on the specification the following are all valid outcomes of goal setting and would gain credit in the exam:

● Improve your training – **for example, a gymnast sets a goal of working hard every training session and this leads to more effective training.**

● Increase your motivation – **for example, a middle-aged man sets a goal of running an extra mile each week and this goal makes him more determined to succeed.**

● Increase your pride and satisfaction – **for example, an elderly woman sets herself a goal of swimming 30 lengths of the swimming pool each week. When she achieves this she feels a sense of pride and satisfaction.**

● Achieve more – **for example, if an athlete sets a goal of winning the next race may find that he does win the race.**

When you set goals try to:

● pace yourself – do not try to do too much too soon.

● give yourself rewards.

● keep goals realistic.

● keep a record of your goals.

● do not feel bad if things do not go well – plan your next step.

## 22.1 Effective goal setting
Revised

● For goal setting to be effective there must be short-term goals leading to longer term goals – **for example, to win the league cup, the netball team may have to concentrate on winning more games away from home.**

## 22.2 The SMART principle of goal setting
Revised

● **S** Specific: if goals are clear and unambiguous they are more likely to be attained – **for example, to improve the serve technique in tennis is a specific goal.**

● **M** Measurable: this is important for monitoring and makes you accountable – **for example, to eat five portions of fruit or vegetables each day is a measurable goal.**

- **A** Agreed: the sharing of goal setting between parents, personal trainer, coach and performer can give a sense of teamwork – **for example, agree with your parents that you will give up smoking so that there is a shared goal that you will give up smoking.**

- **R** Realistic: motivation will improve if goals can actually be reached – **for example, an obese person starts exercising by going on short walks to start with, which is a realistic goal.**

- **T** Timed: the splitting up of goals into short-term goals that are planned and progressive – **for example, a hockey team has set a goal of at least drawing in the next league game on Saturday.**

**Exam tip**

Be able to identify each element of SMART goals and use a practical example.

## Check your understanding
Tested

1 Explain the SMART principle of goal setting and describe why goal setting is important for an active, healthy lifestyle. *(6 marks)*

2 Which one of the following is a valid reason for setting goals? *(1 mark)*

   a) To try to keep to an exercise programme.

   b) To try to be lucky in a match.

   c) To decrease self-esteem.

   d) To reduce skill levels.

3 SMART target setting is often used to improve performance in physical activities. Which one of the following does the **S** in the SMART principle stand for? *(1 mark)*

   a) Superficial

   b) Standardised

   c) Specific

   d) Special.

# 23. The skeletal system

## 23.1 The functions of the skeleton as part of a healthy active body

Revised

The skeleton has five major functions:

● To give shape and support to the body, thereby giving posture to the body – **for example:**

- **to keep a good posture to prevent backache.**
- **when an athlete has to form a body shape to throw the discuss effectively.**

● To allow movement of the body, by providing areas or sites for muscle attachment. This also provides for a system of levers that help us move – **for example:**

- **for us to be able to carry out everyday activities such as picking things up and moving.**
- **when participating in physical activities such as jogging we need to be able to use levers that our skeletal system provides in order to run.**

● To give protection to the internal organs, such as heart, lungs, spinal cord and the brain – **for example:**

- **the rib cage protects internal organs such as the heart.**
- **the skull or cranium protects the brain.**

● To produce red and white blood cells – **for example:**

- **produces red blood cells that carry much-needed oxygen to make our muscles work.**
- **to produce white blood cells that fight infection and keep the body healthy.**

● To act as a mineral store for minerals such as phosphorus, calcium, potassium, manganese, magnesium, silica, iron, zinc, etc. – **for example:**

- **iron helps in the transport of oxygen to moving muscles during physical activities.**
- **calcium is needed to build and repair bones and to keep us healthy.**

## 23.2 The structure of the skeleton

Revised

Top-level students may also find it useful to understand more about the structure of the skeleton.

● The axial skeleton is the main source of support and is the central part of the skeleton. It includes the cranium, the vertebral column and the rib cage, including twelve pairs of ribs and the sternum.

● The appendicular skeleton consists of the remaining bones and includes the girdles that join these bones on to the axial skeleton.

> **Exam tip**
>
> All the functions of the skeleton listed above need to be learned, along with practical examples of these functions in action both for movement and to keep healthy.
>
> Learn the bones that form the three joints named in the specification – the elbow, knee and shoulder joints.

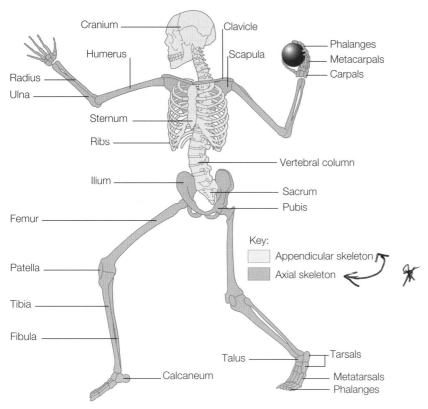

Cranium — Clavicle
Humerus — Scapula
Radius — Phalanges
Ulna — Metacarpals
Carpals
Sternum —
Ribs —
Vertebral column
Ilium — Sacrum
Pubis
Femur —
Patella —
Tibia —
Fibula —
Talus — Tarsals
Calcaneum — Metatarsals
Phalanges

Key:
 Appendicular skeleton
 Axial skeleton

⬆ **Figure 23.1**

## Check your understanding                                    Tested

1 Which of the following bones meet to form the elbow
   joint?                                                      *(1 mark)*

   **a)** Femur and pelvis

   **b)** Humerus and femur

   **c)** Humerus, radius and ulna

   **d)** Humerus, tibia and fibula.

2 Which of the following is an example of the skeleton as a
   support structure?                                          *(1 mark)*

   **a)** Producing red blood cells

   **b)** Storing minerals

   **c)** Producing calcium for strong bones

   **d)** Helping with correct posture.

3 Describe the main functions of the skeletal system that keep the
   body healthy and active.                                    *(5 marks)*

# 24. Joints

- Synovial or freely moveable joints consist of a joint capsule lined with a synovial membrane. There is lubrication provided for the joint in the form of synovial fluid. This is secreted into the joint by the synovial membrane – **for example, the knee joint.**
- The functions of synovial fluid are to:
  - lubricate the joint.
  - protect (for example, cartilage).
  - nourish the cartilage with nutrients.
  - help to stabilise the joint and keeps the joint steady.
- **Hinge joint:** This allows movement in one plane only (uniaxial) – for example, the knee joint. **An example of a physical activity that uses this joint is sprinting when the knee joint allows the flexion and extension of the lower leg.**
- **Ball and socket joint:** This allows a wide range of movement and occurs when a round head of bone fits into a cupped shaped depression – for example, the shoulder joint. **An example of a physical activity that uses this joint is an athlete throwing a javelin when the shoulder joint allows the upper arm to move effectively.**

**Exam tip**

The two types of synovial joint named in the specification are:
- the hinge joint – for example, the elbow and the knee
- the ball and socket joint – for example, the shoulder joint.

You need to be able to identify an example of each and to describe a movement that is associated with the use of each of these two joints.

## 24.1 Cartilage                                    Revised ☐

- This is soft connective tissue.
- Cartilage has no blood supply but receives nutrition though diffusion from the surrounding capillary network.
- White fibro-cartilage consists of tough tissue that acts as a shock absorber. It is found in parts of the body where there is a great amount of stress – for example, in the knee joint.
- Cartilage does not heal very well once it is torn. This is mainly because it does not have a good blood supply.

↑ **Figure 24.1 The thrower needs a healthy and strong shoulder joint, which is a ball and socket joint.**

Unit B453 Developing Knowledge in Physical Education

## 24.2 Ligaments

Revised

- These join bone to bone.
- They are bands of connective tissue that are very tough and resilient.
- The ligaments prevent movements that are extreme and help to stop dislocation.

## 24.3 Associated problems with joints and how to avoid them through an active, healthy lifestyle

Revised

- Arthritis – means inflammation of the joints.
- Most people with arthritis will experience pain and difficulty moving around.
- You can take control of your symptoms by following a healthy lifestyle and thus continue to have a good quality of life.
- Two of the most common forms of arthritis are osteoarthritis and rheumatoid arthritis.
- Osteoarthritis is usually a result of ageing.

The following are not specifically mentioned on the specification, however they would gain you credit in the exam:

- Rheumatoid arthritis (RA) is when a person's immune system attacks cells within the joint capsule.
- If you smoke or are obese then this increases your chances of getting RA.

## 24.4 How to avoid joint problems

Revised

- Keeping to your ideal weight – eat a balanced healthy diet.
- Don't do too much activity at any one time – have rest intervals when appropriate.
- Keep a good posture.
- Wear shoes that have plenty of cushioning – especially when exercising.

## Check your understanding

Tested

1  Explain the function of synovial fluid in joints.  *(3 marks)*

2  Which of the following would you recommend to prevent inflammation of the joints during or after physical activity?  *(1 mark)*

   a) Rub massage oil into your joints before and after exercise.

   b) Use carbo-loading to increase energy levels.

   c) Stretch your muscles thoroughly before exercise.

   d) Do not do too much activity at any one time.

3  What value is cartilage in trying to maintain an active, healthy lifestyle?  *(1 mark)*

   a) Protects bones from wear and tear.

   b) Gives strength to a joint.

   c) Produces valuable red blood cells.

   d) Acts as a nutrient to bones.

# 25. Muscles and movement

## 25.1 The functions of specific muscles

Revised ☐

- Triceps: this is the elbow extensor (*triceps brachii*) and is attached to the elbow. Its function is to straighten the elbow – **for example, backhand in table tennis.**
- Biceps: this is an elbow flexor (*biceps brachii*). Its function is to swing the upper arm forward and to turn the forearm so that the palm of the hand points upwards (supination) – **for example, the biceps curl in weight training.**
- Deltoid: this is used in all movements of the arms. Its most important function is to lift the arm straight outwards and upwards (abduction) – **for example, to make a block in volleyball with arms straight above the head.**
- Pectorals: there are two sets of chest muscle. These help to adduct the arm and rotate it inwards as well as lowering the shoulder blades – **for example, a rugby player making a tackle would hold on to their opponent using the pectoral muscles.**
- Trapezius: this adducts and rotates the shoulder blade outwards. It also helps to turn the head and bends the neck backwards – **for example, a rugby forward in a scrum will use the trapezius to bind into the opponents.**
- Gluteals: these are the muscles in your buttocks. They straighten and adduct the hip, rotate the thigh outwards and helps to straighten the knee – **for example, a sprinter will use the gluteals in the leg action of sprinting down the track.**
- Quadriceps: this provides stability to the knee joint and extends or straightens the knee joint – **for example, a long jumper when driving off the board will straighten the knee joint at take off using the quadriceps.**
- Hamstrings: these muscles will straighten the hip. They will also bend the knee and rotate it outwards – **for example, a hockey player when running across the pitch will be using her hamstrings in the running action to bend the knees.**
- *Gastrocnemius* – or calf muscle, is used to bend the knee and to straighten or plantar flex the ankle – **for example, a swimmer doing front crawl will point their toes in the leg action using the gastrocnemius.**
- *Latissimusdorsi* – the broad back muscle, will swing the arm backwards and rotate it inwards – **for example, a tennis player who when serving swings their arm back to hit the ball is using the latissimusdorsi.**
- Abdominals – these bend the trunk forwards and help to turn the upper body – **for example, performing a sit-up exercise will use the abdominals.**

### Exam tip

Make sure you can:
- identify ways in which an active, healthy lifestyle can maintain and develop the health of muscles
- apply these to practical examples
- explain the role of the major muscle groups in movements.

## 25.2 Pairs of muscles

Revised ☐

- To produce movements, muscles either shorten, lengthen or they remain the same length when they contract.
- Muscles work in pairs. As one muscle contracts, the other relaxes. Muscles that work together like this are called antagonistic pairs.

Examples of antagonistic pairs are:

- Biceps and triceps – at the arm joint. As the biceps bends the arms by contacting, the triceps relax. As the arm straightens, the opposite occurs.
- Hamstrings and quadriceps – at the knee joint. The hamstrings contract and the quadriceps relax and the knee bends. As the knee straightens, the quads contract and the hamstrings relax.

- Agonist – this is the muscle that produces the desired joint movement and is also known as the prime mover – **for example, the biceps brachii is the muscle that produces the flexion movement at the elbow.**
- Antagonist – for movement to be coordinated, muscles work in pairs so that control is maintained. The movement caused by the agonist is countered by the action of the opposing muscle called the antagonist – **for example, the action at the elbow caused by the biceps shortening is opposed by the lengthening of the triceps, which acts as the antagonist.**

## Synergists

- These refer to muscles that are actively helping the prime mover or agonist to produce the desired movement.
- Ranges of movement – **for example, the brachialis acts as a synergist when the elbow is bent and the forearm moves upwards.**

## 25.3 Ranges of movement

Revised

- **Flexion** is a decrease in the angle around a joint – **for example, bend your arm at the elbow and touch your shoulder with your hand.**
- **Extension:** This is when the angle of the bones that are moving (articulating bones) is increased – **for example, from a stooped or squat position you then stand up. The angle between your femur and tibia (upper and lower leg) increases, thus extension has taken place.**
- **Abduction:** The movement of the body away from the middle or the midline of the body – **for example, lying on your left side and lifting your right leg straight up away from the midline.**
- **Adduction:** this is the opposite of abduction and is the movement towards the midline – **for example, lowering your lifted leg that you have abducted towards the middle of your body.**
- **Rotation:** This is when the bone turns about its longitudinal axis within the joint – **for example, a ballet dancer moves into first position and rotates the hip joint.**

## Check your understanding

Tested

1 Which of the following movements best describes flexion around a joint? *(1 mark)*

   a) Lowering your body using your arms in the press-up position.

   b) Bending backwards at the hip whilst standing.

   c) Turning your hand around so that the palm is facing upwards.

   d) Squeezing your ankles together whilst lying on the floor.

2 Identify **two** major muscle groups of the upper body that are used when performing a standing throw of a ball. Explain how an active lifestyle can keep muscles healthy. *(5 marks)*

3 Which one of the following is an example of a hinge joint? *(1 mark)*

   a) The shoulder joint

   b) The hip joint

   c) The knee joint

   d) The wrist joint.

# 26. Tendons and the effects of lactic acid

## 26.1 Tendons

- Tendons attach muscles to bones.
- These are strong and can be a little flexible and they help to apply the power needed to move bones.
- If contraction is excessively strong then tendons can be damaged. **For example, the Achilles tendon is found in the lower leg and can be damaged.**
- Exercise without strain can strengthen tendons and make them more flexible and less prone to injury.
- Tendonitis means inflammation of a tendon.
- Symptoms are: tenderness; pain; swelling; movement being reduced in muscle/s that are pulled by the inflamed tendon/s.
- If you exercise excessively then some areas of the body are more prone to tendonitis – **for example, tendons over the wrist and hand are the most commonly affected if you play a lot of squash.**

### How to avoid problems with tendons

- Avoid repetitive movements and overuse of the affected area.
- Do exercises to strengthen the muscles around the affected tendon.
- Seek medical advice if appropriate.
- Rest the affected part.
- The use of ice packs over the affected area may ease swelling and pain.

> **Exam tip**
> The specification states that associated problems with tendons need to be described as well as how to avoid them.

## 26.2 The effects of lactic acid

- With the absence of oxygen lactic acid is formed in the working muscles.
- Lactic acid causes muscle pain and often this leads us to stop or reduce the activity we are doing.
- We cannot use the **anaerobic** system for long because of this build up of lactic acid.
- When we recover, we take in oxygen and this helps to convert lactic acid into waste products that we can get rid of it.

An active healthy lifestyle will:

- improve the muscles' capability of using oxygen more efficiently.
- help muscles deal with larger amounts of lactic acid.
- ensure that we can keep going for longer in activities and physical work.
- help avoid illness and disease.

> **Exam tip**
> The specification states that you need to know how lactic acid can affect exercise and training and the ability to keep going.

1  Which one of the following is an effect of lactic acid during an
   exercise session?                                        *(1 mark)*

   a) Helps you focus on the exercise task.

   b) Causes muscle fatigue during exercise.

   c) Causes stomach ache due to over-eating.

   d) Helps to break down oxygen to produce more energy.

2  Which one of the following best describes the role of
   tendons?                                                 *(1 mark)*

   a) They attach muscles to bones.

   b) They attach muscles to muscles.

   c) They attach bones to bones.

   d) They attach ligaments to bones.

3  Why is lactic acid produced in our muscles? Briefly describe the
   effects of lactic acid.                                  *(4 marks)*

# 27. Mental preparation

You can control emotions by:

- Relaxing mentally – **for example, controlling anxiety in a volleyball competition.**

- Trying to be more confident – **for example, a hockey captain giving a half-time talk to the team.**

- Ignore the crowd and focus on what you are doing – **for example, being focused when about to perform a gymnastic routine.**

The rest of these ways of controlling emotion are not mentioned explicitly on the specification but would get you marks in the exam:

- Keeping calm or 'chilled' or controlling **arousal** – **for example, calming down before a sprint race.**

- Not getting carried away or over-excited – **for example, trying to calm down before a football match.**

- Not criticising others – **for example, if your team-mate misses a penalty you encourage them.**

- Trying to see other people's point of view – **for example, understanding that the referee is trying to do his best and is fair.**

- Showing etiquette or sportsmanship – **for example, clapping your opponent when they play a good tennis match.**

- Using imagery or use mental rehearsal – **for example, a netball player visualises shooting at the goal before she shoots.**

> **Exam tip**
>
> You may be asked to explain how mental preparation can:
> - control emotions
> - enable you to play sport and exercise fairly
> - help you cope with stress.

## 27.1 Mental-preparation techniques

Revised ☐

These are widely used by those who participate in all kinds of physical activities as well as by sportsmen and women to cope with high levels of anxiety.

- Controlling the heart rate by relaxation methods can make us feel more positive about performing.

- Imagery can improve concentration and confidence – **for example, a winter Olympic athlete who is responsible for steering the team's bobsleigh visualises or uses imagery to picture the track, with all its bends, twists and turns.**

  - Imagery can also help with relaxation.

- Self-talk is a technique that involves the participant in a physical activity or sports performer being positive about past experiences and performances and future efforts by talking to themselves.

  - This technique has been shown to help with self-confidence and to raise levels of aspiration.

- Relaxation: the more physically relaxed you can get, the more mentally relaxed you can be. There is, of course, a happy medium in physical activities – you don't want to be too laid back because you often need to react quickly and dynamically.

  - Relaxation exercises can be very useful before you attempt to train yourself in mental exercises such as imagery.

- This helps the sports person to be **calmer** and **steadier** before performance.
- Relaxation skills are like any other type of skill, you need to **practise** hard to **achieve** them.

## Check your understanding

1 Describe how emotions can be controlled when participating in physical activities. *(5 marks)*

2 Mental preparation is important when participating in physical activity. Which one of the following best describes the purpose of mental preparation for a young person who is exercising to keep generally fit? *(1 mark)*

   **a)** To psych yourself up to win and be competitive.

   **b)** To concentrate effort and forget about stressful events.

   **c)** To focus on one particular muscle group and to build muscle.

   **d)** To block out the crowd.

3 Describe, using practical examples, how the control of emotions can help with the management of stress in physical activities. *(4 marks)*

4 Describe the effects of mental preparation on the performance of physical activities. *(4 marks)*

# 28. Short-term effects of exercise

## 28.1 The cardiovascular system

Revised ☐

The following are short-term responses to exercise related to the cardiovascular system:

- The heart rate increases.
- More blood is pumped to working muscles.
- Blood is redirected and the vascular shunt mechanism operates – more blood is pumped to the working muscles and less blood goes to organs that do not need oxygen.

↑ **Figure 28.1**

- Cardiac output increases – this is the volume of blood that is pumped out of the heart from one ventricle per minute.
- Stroke volume increases – this is the volume of blood pumped out of the heart per beat.

## 28.2 The respiratory system

Revised ☐

- Breathing rate rises – due to demands for more oxygen.
- Tidal volume (TV) – increases during exercise. This is the volume of air either inspired or expired per breath.
- Minute volume – increases during exercise. This is the volume of air that is inspired or expired in one minute.

### Exam tip

The examiner will not be asking any detailed questions about volumes but will ask about how these are affected by exercise both in the short term and the long term.

## 28.3 The muscular system

Revised ☐

- Increase in muscle fatigue.
- Increase in muscle temperature.
- Increased flexibility around the joints. (This point is not explicit on the specification, but is a valid response of the muscular system to exercise and therefore would gain credit in the exam.)

1  Which one of the following best describes the vascular shunt mechanism? *(1 mark)*

   a) Speeding up the flow of blood to all organs during exercise.

   b) The redistribution of blood during exercise.

   c) The pushing forward of waste products to help excretion.

   d) An increase in heart rate that increases cardiac output.

2  Which one of the following is a short-term effect on the heart during an exercise session? *(1 mark)*

   a) Lower resting heart rate.

   b) Increase in tidal volume.

   c) Hypertrophy of the heart muscle.

   d) Increase in cardiac output.

3  Give **three** short-term effects of exercise on the heart. *(3 marks)*

4  Describe three short-term effects of exercise on the respiratory system. *(3 marks)*

# 29. Long-term effects of exercise

## 29.1 The cardiovascular system
Revised

- Lower resting heart rate. This enables us to do more each day and to carry out longer and harder exercise.
- Increase in **stroke volume** at rest and during exercise. This will enable more oxygen to be used by our working muscles and organs.
- **Cardiac output** increases. This, again, will enable us to be more energetic and healthy.

The following long-term effects of exercise on the cardio-vascular system are not explicitly referred to on the specification, but would gain you marks in the exam:

- Size of heart increases – called cardiac hypertrophy. This will make our heart healthier and ward off the onset of heart disease.
- Increase in blood capillaries, which enables a higher oxygen uptake.
- Blood capillaries become more efficient and therefore can provide us with more energy throughout the day.
- Decrease in resting blood pressure, which will help to offset disease and keep us healthy.
- Increase in **haemoglobin**, which helps carry oxygen along with an increase in red blood cells. The more oxygen that is available, the more work we can carry out and for longer.

## 29.2 The respiratory system
Revised

- Increase in lung volumes or vital capacity. This enables us to uptake more oxygen, which will, again, give us more energy throughout the day.
- More rapid rate of recovery – we can recover much faster after a programme of regular exercise.

## 29.3 The muscular system
Revised

- Muscles get bigger.
- Muscles get stronger and can achieve a greater force of movement.
- **Aerobic** adaptations in muscle. Activities like swimming or running can enlarge slow-twitch fibres, which gives greater potential for energy production.
- **Anaerobic** adaptations in muscle. Activities like sprinting or weight lifting can cause fast-twitch muscle fibres to enlarge. This will strengthen our muscles and make them more efficient.
- Muscle cells enable more oxygen to be used by our working muscles. Therefore more energy is available and more work can be done.

- The onset of fatigue is delayed because of higher maximum oxygen uptake (VO2 max.). This will enable us to work harder and for longer, and not to tire too quickly.
- Improved flexibility of the muscle, which enables a greater range of movement. (Again, although this is not mentioned directly on the specification, it is a valid point and would be creditworthy in the exam.)

## Check your understanding

1 Which one of the following is a long-term effect of a healthy, active lifestyle? *(1 mark)*

   a) Heart rate increases.

   b) Muscles increase in temperature.

   c) Blood flow is slower.

   d) Stroke volume increases.

2 Explain, using practical examples, how a healthy, active lifestyle can maintain and develop the health of muscles. *(5 marks)*

3 There are many long-term effects of exercise and training on the body. Which one of the following is a long-term effect on the heart? *(1 mark)*

   a) Increase in stroke volume.

   b) Decrease in stroke volume.

   c) Increase in tidal volume.

   d) Decrease in tidal volume.

4 Describe **four** long-term effects of exercise on muscles. *(4 marks)*

# 30. Exercise and training principles

The age of the participant, time available, equipment available and skill level must all be taken into consideration before the following principles of training are applied.

**Exam tip**

The examiner will be looking for you to be able to name each principle and how it can be used to improve fitness.

## 30.1 Principles of training

Revised

### Specificity

- The training undertaken should be **specific** and relevant to the appropriate needs of the activity or the type of sport involved. **For example, a sprinter would carry out more anaerobic training because the event is mostly anaerobic in nature.**

### Overload

- The need to work the body harder than normal so that there is some stress and discomfort.
- Adaptation and progress will follow overload because the body will respond by adapting to the stress experienced. **For instance, in weight training the lifter will eventually attempt heavier weights or an increase in repetitions, thus overloading the body.**
- Overload can be achieved by a combination of increasing the **frequency, the intensity and the duration** of the activity.

### Progression

- Training should progressively become more difficult.
- Once adaptations have occurred, then the performer should make even more demands on the body.
- It is important that progression does not mean 'overdoing it'. Training must be sensibly progressive and realistic if it is to be effective, otherwise injury may occur.

### Reversibility

- Performance can deteriorate if training stops or decreases in intensity for any length of time.
- If training is stopped, then the fitness gained will be largely lost. For instance, stamina and muscle strength can decrease.

### Variance

A and A* students might also wish to remember the following, for extra marks:

- There should be variety in training methods.
- If training is too predictable, then performers can become demotivated and bored.
- Overuse injuries are also common when training is too repetitive with one muscle group or part of the body, therefore variance can also help prevent injury.

The 'FITT' method of ensuring that training adheres to the principles of training. FITT stands for:

- **F** = frequency of training (number of training sessions each week). This will depend on the level of ability and fitness of the performer. **The elite athlete will train every day, whereas the lower level club player may train only once per week.**

- **I** = Intensity of the exercise undertaken or how hard you work. This will, again, take into account the individual differences of the performer and the type of training being undertaken. **It is suggested that there should be a training intensity of 60–75 per cent of maximal heart rate reserve for the average athlete.**

- **T** = Time or duration that the training takes up. **If aerobic training is required, this should be a minimum of 20 minutes or so.**

- **T** = Type of training to be considered that fulfils specific needs. The type of sport or your role in that sport will dictate what type of training you follow. **For example, a triathlete will train in all areas of fitness but pay particular attention to aerobic and muscular endurance because of the nature of the sport. For archery the type of training might include aspects of muscular endurance to keep muscles steady for effective aiming.**

> **Exam tip**
>
> The specification demands that you know what FITT stands for and that you can give a practical example for each element and how it might affect health and fitness.

## Check your understanding

Tested

1  Which one of the following is the best description of the specificity training principle whilst weight training? *(1 mark)*

   a) Increase the weights lifted for each training session.

   b) Concentrate on training muscles in the upper body.

   c) Lifting your maximum weight for one repetition.

   d) Using all free weights rather than machines.

2  Which one of the following best describes the frequency element of the FITT principle of training? *(1 mark)*

   a) How hard you exercise.

   b) The type of exercise you choose.

   c) How much time you take to exercise.

   d) How many times a week you exercise.

3  The main training principles are: overload; specificity; progression and reversibility. Describe three of these training principles and give a practical example for each. *(3 marks)*

# 31. Aerobic and anaerobic exercise and training

## 31.1 Aerobic exercise
Revised

- This is when the body is working **with** the presence of oxygen.
- Aerobic capacity can be improved through continuous, steady state (sub-maximal) training.
- This low-intensity exercise must take place over a long period of time from 20 minutes to 2 hours.
- The intensity of this exercise should be 60–80 per cent of your maximum heart rate.
- **For example, this type of exercise enables you to be able to finish an exercise routine or to keep up with your friends when walking home from school.**

## 31.2 Anaerobic exercise
Revised

- This is when the body is working **without** the presence of oxygen.
- Training involves high-intensity work.
- This type of activity can only be carried out for a short amount of time because of the lack of oxygen and the build-up of lactic acid – **for example, lifting something quickly off the floor or doing an activity such as sprinting for a ball.**

**Exam tip**

The specification demands only simple descriptions of aerobic and anaerobic exercise, along with examples of each.

## 31.3 Types of training
Revised

### Circuit training – mostly anaerobic but could incorporate aerobic training

- This involves a series of exercises that are arranged in a particular way called a circuit because the training involves repetition of each activity.
- For effective training different, muscle groups should be worked on, with no two muscle-groups being worked on one after the other. **For instance, an activity that uses the main muscle groups in the arms should then be followed, for example, by an exercise involving the muscle groups in the legs.**
- The types of exercises that are involved in circuit training are press-ups, star jumps, dips and squat thrusts.
- Circuit training can also incorporate skills in the activities. **For example, hockey players might include dribbling activities, flicking the ball, shuttle runs and shooting activities.**

### Weight and resistance training methods – mostly anaerobic training

- For strength to be developed, more resistance can be used in the form of weight training or against other types of resistance (such as the use of pulleys).
- Weight training involves a number of repetitions and sets, depending on the type of strength that needs to be developed. **For throwing events in athletics, for example, training methods must involve very high resistance and low repetition. For strength endurance that you may need in swimming or cycling, more repetitions need to be involved with less resistance or lighter weights.**

## Plyometrics – mostly anaerobic training

● This type of training is designed to improve dynamic strength or power.
● Plyometrics improves the speed in which muscles shorten. **Anyone playing a sport that involves sprinting, throwing and jumping will benefit from this type of training, as will players of many team sports like netball or rugby.**
● Plyometrics involves, bounding, hopping and jumping, when muscles have to work concentrically (jumping up) and eccentrically (landing).

## Flexibility training

● It involves stretching exercises of the muscles.
● It can help with performance by enabling a greater range of movement.
● It can improve speed because muscles can work over a greater range.
● It helps to avoid injury by making muscles more supple and enabling a greater range of movement around the joints.

## Continuous training – aerobic training

● Training to maintain and improve aerobic endurance is to take part in endurance-based training.
● Activities such as jogging or swimming can be very beneficial for aerobic endurance.
● This should be carried out at a steady rate or with low intensity – between 20–30 minutes to 2 hours.

## Fartlek training – good for aerobic and anaerobic training

● This training is good for aerobic fitness because it is an endurance activity.
● It is good for anaerobic fitness because of the speed activities undertaken over a short period of time.
● Throughout the exercise, the speed and intensity of the training is varied. **In a one-hour session, for instance, there may be walking activity that is low in intensity to very fast sprinting, which is high intensity.**

## Interval training – can improve both aerobic and anaerobic fitness.

● It is called interval training because there are intervals of work and intervals of rest.
● For training the aerobic system, there should be slower intervals, which makes it suitable for sports like athletics and swimming and for team games like hockey or football.
● For training the anaerobic system, there should be shorter, more intense, intervals of training.

## Check your understanding
Tested ☐

1 Which one of the following best describes aerobic training? *(1 mark)*

   a) Long intervals of slow work    c) Long intervals of fast work
   b) Short intervals of slow work    d) Short intervals of fast work

2 Which one of the following training methods is mostly aerobic? *(1 mark)*

   a) Circuit training      c) Continuous training
   b) Weight training      d) Flexibility training

3 Which one of the following statements best describes aerobic training? *(1 mark)*

   a) Long intervals of moderate exercise
   b) Short sharp sprints with long rest intervals
   c) Lifting heavy weights with few repetitions
   d) Plyometric exercises over short intervals

4 Describe what is meant by aerobic and anaerobic exercise and give practical examples for each. *(4 marks)*

# 32. Potential hazards

## 32.1 Types of hazard
Revised

### Poor physical fitness or inappropriate physique for the activity

● Physical activities require at least some level of fitness of the participant. **For example, to be involved in gymnastics you need to have some flexibility and the ability to be able to support your own weight.**

### Poor level of skill or technique

● There are many cases of injury caused through inexperience. Some players new to physical activities and sport will not know how to participate safely. **For example, more injuries sustained in hockey at lower ability levels relate to inappropriate use of the hockey stick.**

### Lack of effective preparation for sport, for example, warming up and cooling down

● It is crucial that all performers in physical activities and sport take appropriate steps to prepare for vigorous activity through an effective warm-up and, following the activity, a cool-down.

### Dangerous training practices

● Some training methods are not properly recognised, which may prove to be dangerous and cause injury or illness. **For example, in gymnastics there have been horrendous spinal injuries caused by pushing young gymnasts too far and getting them to attempt moves that they are not ready for – with disastrous consequences.**

### Dangerous environment – for example, broken bottles on a playing field

● Large stones, broken glass and even discarded hypodermic syringe needles can cause serious injury. **Another example would be an exercise class held in a church hall, where there may well be chairs stacked around the outside that may fall and potentially cause injury.**

### Weather conditions

● Severe hot weather can cause dehydration and heat exhaustion and severe cold weather can cause hypothermia.

● If there is a thunderstorm there is a risk of being struck by lightning, especially in water-based activities.

### Inappropriate or dangerous clothing

● Certain items of clothing can be dangerous if they get in the way of safe activity – **for example, training shoes must be correctly laced to avoid them coming off.**

### Jewellery

● This should not be worn if you are participating in activities where others may hurt. **For example, other people can be hurt by rings or the sports participant could get a necklace caught in the clothing of an opponent and then experience a serious cut to the neck.**

> **Exam tip**
> Hazards can *cause* injury but they are not injuries – for example, concussion is not a hazard but a low metal beam in a sports centre *is* a hazard.

## Lifting and carrying of equipment

● There are many instances of back strains and even broken limbs caused by incorrect methods of lifting and carrying sports equipment.

## Inappropriate or damaged equipment

● The equipment that is used in physical activity and sport should also be correct for the activity and the age/ability of the people involved. **For example, in gymnastics the vaulting box should be at an appropriate height.**

## Behaviour of other participants

● The correct way of behaving in physical activity and sport is important to prevent injury. **For example, if a child throws a discus out of turn then this may well hit another child, thereby causing a nasty injury.**

### Exam tip

The examiner may ask for examples of hazards in a particular situation:

● the gymnasium, sports hall or fitness centre.

● the playing field

● an artificial outdoor area

● court areas

● outdoor adventurous areas.

The examiner may also link the hazard to a role, for example, for a participant, leader or official.

## Check your understanding — Tested

1 Which one of the following is a potential hazard whilst participating in a physical activity in an outdoor adventure area? *(1 mark)*

   **a)** Slippery rocks. ✓

   **b)** Cutting your leg on a sharp stone.

   **c)** Concussion by banging your head.

   **d)** Exhaustion because of walking too far.

2 Which one of the following is **not** a hazard found on a grass playing field? *(1 mark)*

   **a)** Broken glass

   **b)** Football posts

   **c)** Concussion ✓

   **d)** Pot holes

3 Which one of the following is a potential hazard in a sports hall? *(1 mark)*

   **a)** Falling over and experiencing concussion.

   **b)** Water that has been spilled causes the floor to be slippery. ✓

   **c)** A twisted ankle playing five-a-side football.

   **d)** Needing a plaster after cutting yourself.

4 Identify **five** potential hazards that may be found in a fitness centre. *(5 marks)*

# 33. Reducing the risks

- Make sure that you are **fit** for physical activity and sport. **For example, in basketball you are required to stretch suddenly so make sure that you have worked on your flexibility to prevent injury.**

- You must get to a particular **skill level** and have good skill technique before performing seriously in physical activity and sport.

- Whatever the level of the physical activity or sport – whether it is serious competition or just recreational play, you should be prepared for the activity by carrying out an effective **warm-up**.

- A **cool-down** is equally important and should take place immediately after exercise.

- Follow **health and safety procedures**. Most activities have health and safety guidelines and as an official you should know what these are – **for example, are the five-a-side goalposts safely anchored in the sports hall?**

- Wear safe clothing. Clothing for physical activity and sport should also be suitable for the activity to provide enough warmth and also to not be hazardous to the owner and others around them.

Top-level students might also want to remember the following, which, although not explicitly on the specification, would also gain you marks in the exam:

- You should also ensure that you **do not push yourself** too hard and that you 'listen' to your body and stop if any exercise hurts or you are getting unduly fatigued.

- Eat and drink correctly: have a balanced diet that ensures that you have all the nutrients and enough water. Drink plenty of water during and after exercise even if you are not very thirsty.

- Don't drink too much alcohol because this interferes with health and fitness levels.

↑ **Figure 33.1 Alcohol negatively affects your health and fitness levels.**

- Don't take any fitness or performance-enhancing drugs – they are, of course, banned and they should never be taken because of their many health risks and because if caught you are likely to be banned from any competitions and from participating.

- Make sure you have a safe environment – any playing surfaces should also be safe. **For example, football pitches should be checked for**

**broken glass or large stones and the basketball court should be dry and not slippery.**

- Use correct lifting and carrying procedures.
- Ensure good personal hygiene.
- Hair should be washed regularly and in many physical activities should be tied back to avoid accidents.
- Nails should be kept thoroughly clean because long nails in particular can harbour many germs. In many physical activities it may be appropriate to have short nails because of the risk of scratching or injuring another participant.
- Skin should be washed or showered after physical activity because of the build-up of sweat that can harbour bacteria and, of course, will also give off an unpleasant odour.
- Feet should also be kept clean and you should change your socks regularly but particularly after physical exercise. Dry them well because feet that are left damp can attract infections such as athlete's foot.
- Clothing should be clean and should be changed regularly and washed and thoroughly dried.

> **Exam tip**
>
> Remember the essentials:
> - Correct clothing
> - Safety equipment
> - Follow health and safety procedures
> - Lift and carry correctly
> - Compete at the right level
> - Warm up and cool down
> - Ensure good personal hygiene.

## Check your understanding                                    Tested ☐

1  How would you minimise the risks associated with a fitness centre when exercising?                                   *(1 mark)*

   **a)** Eat plenty of carbohydrates.

   **b)** Check that all equipment is working properly.

   **c)** Always try hard in all exercises.

   **d)** Record fitness progress in your training diary.

2  Which one of the following would be a good example of personal protective equipment to reduce the risk of injury if participating in a physical activity?                       *(1 mark)*

   **a)** A gum shield in hockey.

   **b)** A post protector in rugby.

   **c)** A crash-barrier for the crowd.

   **d)** Well-fitting training shoes.

3  Describe ways in which you might reduce the potential risks in outdoor, adventurous activities.                          *(5 marks)*

# 34. Effects of media and sponsorship

## 34.1 Media influences Revised

- There are often features on the news and current affairs programmes that relate to healthy lifestyles – **for example, healthy eating or giving up smoking or reducing the consumption of alcohol.**
- The media can also be guilty of reinforcing unhealthy lifestyles through characters in dramas and soaps.

### Positive aspects of the media

- Often promotes sport and exercise.
- Can promote healthy living by informing us of its benefits – **for example, a documentary about healthy eating.**
- Motivates you to follow a healthy lifestyle through role models or sports stars.
- Promotional campaigns related to health via public service broadcasting.
- Showing a wide variety of activities on some channels.
- Has led to more money being raised for health campaigns.

### Negative aspects of the media

- May reinforce unhealthy lifestyle and encourage alcohol consumption or smoking.
- Too much use of the media discourages activity and can lead to the 'couch potato' syndrome.
- Minority sports are often under-represented.
- Women's sport and activity is under-represented.
- Not much disability sport.

### Promotional campaigns

- Promotional campaigns for healthy behaviour are often used as part of the media's role in public service broadcasting.
- Mass-media health promotion campaigns are used to educate the public about such health issues.
- The media also includes the Internet and there are a number of websites that promote healthy lifestyles.

## 34.2 Effects of sponsorship and funding in being able to follow an active healthy lifestyle Revised

### Funding

- Grants are made available to public and voluntary sectors usually.
- Many grants involve the sports organisation putting forward a percentage of the funds themselves.

- Sometimes there are subsidies whereby the members of public pay a certain cost and the local authority pays the rest.
- Membership fees: most sports organisations have membership fees – **for example, to join a hockey club an annual membership fee is paid**.
- The National Lottery. This is used partly as a grant for sport. World-class performers are funded also through the lottery. UK Sport is lottery funded and this, in turn, funds high performance sport in the UK.

## Sponsorship

- The exercise and sport market is now big business, with large amounts of money being spent by commercial companies on sports' participants and events – **for example, a company such as Adidas might sponsor a top-class tennis player to wear a particular style of training shoe**.
- At the other end of the scale, a local hockey club may attract a small amount of money to go towards the first team kit.
- There has also been a significant increase in sponsorship due to sports clothing being fashionable – **for example, there has been a huge increase in sales of training shoes**.
- Commercial companies recognise that top sports stars can be fashion role models for the young and therefore use them in advertising campaigns.
- There is a lack of sponsorship for the 'middle-ranking sports'. Many sports are unable to attract sponsors because they cannot get television coverage.
- Sponsors continue to seek image enhancement and brand awareness through sponsorship.
- Sponsors are also looking to sell their products and develop promotional opportunities.
- Women's sport has fewer sponsors.

↑ Figure 34.1 The media has both positive and negative effects for sponsorship.

## Check your understanding

Tested ☐

1 Which one of the following is an example of a media promotional campaign to promote a healthy, active lifestyle? *(1 mark)*

   a) TV advertisement for high-energy drinks.

   b) Radio advertisement for sportswear.

   c) Leaflets on a balanced diet in the local library.

   d) Newspaper report on a death caused by smoking.

2 Which one of the following is an example of sponsorship? *(1 mark)*

   a) TV advertising for a sports drink.

   b) Health campaign in the local newspaper.

   c) A drinks company giving money for a fun run event.

   d) Money paid to a professional footballer by his club.

3 Explain how the media influences those who participate in physical activities. *(6 marks)*

# 35. Local and national provision

## 35.1 Role of the local authority in promoting physical activities

Revised ☐

- Local authorities recognise the benefits of developing physical activity and sport for their community and to ensure an overall better quality of life.
- Local authorities will also help in the development of sports facilities, both with financial help and also with advice about strategy and building regulations.
- Local authorities will often run coach-education programmes, including coaching courses for all levels of prospective coaches.
- To increase participation and interest in sport, local authorities will run 'taster sessions' in sports, summer schools and competitions and tournaments in a wide variety of sports.

> **Exam tip**
>
> Describe the role of the local authority in promoting participation or leading or officiating in physical activities.

## 35.2 Role of private enterprise in promoting physical activities

Revised ☐

- The private sector is involved in physical activities and sports development by getting as many involved as possible, to raise attendance levels and to improve their profits.
- The private sector, unlike the voluntary sector, has the motivation to make money both in terms of the organisation and those that run the organisation. **An example of a private club would be a Health and Fitness Club that provides equipment and instruction in health, fitness and often beauty activities, as well as the increasingly important area of personal training.**

## 35.3 Role of voluntary organisations in promoting physical activities

Revised ☐

- Volunteers and their organisations continue to be a very important aspect in the running of physical activities and sport in the UK. There are estimated to be more than six million people involved in the voluntary sector in physical activities and sport.
- The people who work in these organisations such as hockey clubs, rambling organisations and climbing and ski associations are rarely paid and the organisations are not profit-making.
- The role of voluntary organisations in physical activities and sports development is that they often support local needs.
- **For example, a local athletics club tries to get as many people to be involved in athletics as possible and tries to attract people of different ages and from different socio-economic backgrounds. This voluntary club would run a team in the local leagues and hold training sessions for their members.**

## 35.4 The role of governing bodies in promoting physical activities

Revised

- For example, the **FA, LTA, ASA, RFU,** etc. There are over 265 governing bodies in the UK.
- The teams and clubs then pay a subscription to the governing body.
- They, in turn, administer the sport nationally and organise competitions and the national team.
- The national governing bodies are also members of international governing bodies – for example, UEFA and FIFA. These international bodies control and organise international competitions.

> **Exam tip**
>
> Be able to name at least three different governing bodies (from the UK only) and link them to the sport they represent – for example, the LTA is the Lawn Tennis Association representing tennis.

## 35.5 The role of Olympic organisations

Revised

### British Olympic Association (BOA)

- Formed in 1905, the BOA supplies the delegates for the National Olympic Committee (NOC).
- The BOA is responsible amongst other things for the planning and execution of the Great Britain Olympic Team's participation in the Olympic and Olympic Winter Games.
- Working with the Olympic Governing Bodies, the BOA selects Team GB from the best sportsmen and women who will go on to compete in the Olympic sports.
- The BOA delivers extensive support services to Britain's Olympic athletes and their National Governing Bodies throughout each Olympic cycle to assist them in their preparations for, and performances at the Games.

### International Olympic Committee (IOC)

- The IOC was created by the Paris Congress in 1894. It owns all the rights to the Olympic symbol and the Games themselves.
- This is the world body that administers the Olympic Movement. Its headquarters are in Lausanne, Switzerland.
- Members are appointed to the IOC and are responsible for selecting the host cities of the Olympic Games, both summer and winter.

> **Exam tip**
>
> Link your knowledge of these organisations (BOA and IOC) to promoting participation.
>
> Government funding has risen by over 800 per cent in the past 10 years to over £400 million a year. Nationally the number of adults doing 3 x 30 minutes of sport and physical activity a week is on the rise.

### Check your understanding

Tested

1 Describe how the British Olympic Association might help you if you were an Olympic athlete. *(3 marks)*

2 Which one of the following is an example of a national governing body? *(1 mark)*

   a) British Olympic Association

   b) UK Sport

   c) Lawn Tennis Association

   d) International Olympic Committee.

3 Give **three** examples of national governing bodies and name the sports they represent. *(3 marks)*

# 36. Government initiatives

The specification states that candidates should be familiar with a range of up-to-date government initiatives, the author has selected some for discussion here but others could be just as valid.

## 36.1 Government Healthy Living Initiative
Revised

- The Government's Healthy Living programme is aimed at promoting healthy living through a range of initiatives aimed at families with young children.
- Young families are aware of the 5 A Day message but are not necessarily eating 5 A Day.

## 36.2 'Top Tips for Top Mums'
Revised

- This is an extension of the highly successful 5 A Day campaign and encourages parents across the country to share tips and ideas with each other on how they get their children to eat more fruit and vegetables.
- Top Tips for Top Mums targets families from low-income backgrounds with young children.
- To get the best benefit from the nutrients packed into fruit and vegetables, everyone should aim for a variety of different types and colours every day.

### Exam tip

You will not be asked about specific initiatives because these are continuously being developed/changed. You *will* be asked to describe your own examples of these initiatives and how they promote active, healthy lifestyles.

## 36.3 Change4Life
Revised

- This is supported by the Department of Health, which aims to improve children's diets and levels of activity thus reducing the threat to their future health and happiness.
- The goal is to help every family in England eat well, move more and live longer.
- A collection of companies including BSkyB, ITV, Tesco, Coca-Cola, Cadbury and AOL have pledged the equivalent of more than £200m in advertising space and services to support the government's 'Change4Life' healthy lifestyles marketing initiative.

## 36.4 Five choices to help you stay healthy
Revised

- **You should not smoke.**
- **Do some regular physical activity** – Anything that gets you mildly out of breath and a little sweaty is fine. **For example, jogging, heavy gardening, swimming, cycling, etc.** A brisk walk each day is what many people do, and that is fine. However, it is thought that the more vigorous the activity, the better. **To gain most benefit you should do at least 30 minutes of physical activity on most days.**
- **Eat a healthy diet.**
- **Try to lose weight if you are overweight or obese.**
- **Don't drink too much alcohol.**

- The aim is to do a mixture of aerobic activities and muscle-strengthening activities.

- Aerobic activities are those that make the heart and lungs work harder. For example: brisk walking, jogging, swimming, cycling, dancing, badminton, tennis, etc. You can even use normal activities as part of your physical activity routine. For example, fairly heavy housework, DIY, or gardening can make you mildly out of breath and mildly sweaty.

- To gain health benefits you should do at least 30 minutes of moderate aerobic physical activity on most days (at least five days per week).

- 30 minutes per day is probably the minimum to gain health benefits.

- Muscle-strengthening activities – adults should aim to do a minimum of two sessions of muscle-strengthening activities per week (not on consecutive days).

- For older people, the same adult recommendations still apply, depending on ability. A particular goal for older people should be, where possible, to maintain or increase flexibility and balance.

- Maintaining flexibility and balance helps older people remain independent, and reduces the risk of falls and injury from falls.

- For children and teenagers there should be at least one hour a day of moderate physical activity. The hour can be made up from various shorter sessions each day – so, it can be achieved by a mixture of play, PE, games, dance, cycling, a brisk walk to school, sports, various outdoor activities, etc.

## Check your understanding

Tested

1 Identify current government initiatives related to healthy eating and exercise. Explain how they might help young people to follow a healthy, active lifestyle. *(6 marks)*

2 Which one of the following is a government initiative to encourage healthy eating? *(1 mark)*

   a) Take brisk walks instead of using a car.

   b) Drink no more than eight units of alcohol per day.

   c) Eat at least five portions of fruit and vegetables per day.

   d) Add salt to food to improve flavour.

# 37. School influences

- Schools provide Physical Education lessons, which encourage the development of skills used in many physical activities and sports.

- Extra-curricular sports activities are also organised. These are activities run by Physical Education departments and individual teachers in schools related to physical activities. They are called extra-curricular because they fall outside normal curriculum or school time. They may run at break, lunch times or after school or at weekends.

- Many schools run school teams for each age group, as well as 'drop in' clubs for pupils to have taster sessions in a variety of activities such as dance, weight training and team sports.

- Schools also forge links with local clubs and activity classes. Coaches and instructors are often asked to come into school and run classes. This enables young people to progress into classes and clubs outside school.

↑ **Figure 37.1 School is a very important factor in learning about and participating in sport.**

- Examination courses in Physical Education have raised the awareness of the role of sport in society.

- Many schools run courses at Key Stages 3, 4 and 5 that result in some sort of qualification. **For example, Junior Sports Leader qualification at Key Stage 3. At Key Stage 4, GCSE PE or BTEC First in sport may be followed. In the sixth form, A level PE or BTEC National in sport may be followed.**

- There are often links between schools and local sports clubs and other recreation providers.

- The National Curriculum is a government list of courses that must be delivered in all state schools from primary schools to the age of 16 in secondary schools. One of the stated aims of the National Curriculum is to get as many children as possible to actively participate in physical activities and sport.

- Physical Education also involves the learning of information related to health, fitness and diet.

- Schools may become Sports Colleges. These 'specialist schools' must have an extensive extra-curricular programme, which includes links with external clubs.

● Schools can run health-awareness programmes to try to promote an active, healthy lifestyle to pupils and students. These programmes involve giving vital information about diet and exercise and how to avoid smoking, drug taking and excessive alcohol consumption.

## Check your understanding

1 Which one of the following is the role of a school in promoting an active, healthy lifestyle? *(1 mark)*

   **a)** Running health-awareness programmes.

   **b)** Checking on sleep patterns.

   **c)** Giving parents advice on health.

   **d)** Ensuring that family housing is appropriate.

2 Explain how examination courses in physical education can help to promote an active, healthy lifestyle. *(4 marks)*

3 Which one of the following is an example of a school extra-curricular activity that promotes an active, healthy lifestyle? *(1 mark)*

   **a)** A fitness club before school starts.

   **b)** The local hockey club using the school facilities.

   **c)** A health-promotion talk in assemblies.

   **d)** A warm-up before every PE lesson.

# Check your understanding answers

## 1. Key concepts, p.4

1. *(4 marks)*

- Expressing ideas – Helping a team-mate with skills/giving an opinion during coaching/telling the exercise trainer about your own idea for exercise/a dancer showing ideas through their movement.
- Solving problems – Deciding on the equipment to be used during icy weather/choosing a rehabilitation exercise for a damaged knee/constructing a gymnastic routine within the confines of the mat area.
- Exploring tactics – Using different defence strategies for different teams/as an official talking to the players and explaining decisions.
- Being effective – Choosing creative moves that score high points in diving/the free-kick routine devised results in a goal.

2. b *(1 mark)*
3. a *(1 mark)*

## 2. Fundamental motor skills, p.6

1. b *(1 mark)*
2. *(4 marks)*

- Running – measured by time, for example, a 100 metre sprint.
- Throwing – measured by distance, for example, the discus.
- Jumping – measured by distance/height, for example, the long jump.
- Kicking – measured by effectiveness, for example, a footballer shooting.
- Catching – measured by effectiveness, for example, a cricket fielder catching the ball from the batsman.
- Hitting – measured by distance/accuracy/end result, for example, a hockey player hitting the ball as a pass to a fellow player.

3. c *(1 mark)*

## 3. Decision making in physical activities, p.8

1. *(4 marks)*

   ### a) Performer

- First example of a decision made by a performer: to pass the ball in rugby.
- Second example of a decision made by a performer: to shoot the ball in netball.

   ### b) Coach or leader

- First example of a decision made by a coach/leader: deciding to have a time out in basketball.
- Second example of a decision made by a coach/leader: substituting a player in a hockey match.

   ### c) Official

- First example of a decision made by an official: indicating that a player is offside in football.
- Second example of a decision made by an official: indicating the time as a table official in basketball.

2. a *(1 mark)*

## 4. Abiding by the rules, etiquette and sportsmanship, p.10

1. a *(1 mark)*
2. *(3 marks)*

- To prevent injury/make the activity less dangerous.
- For fair play/so that the activity/game can be played fairly, effectively and in a flowing way.
- So all can enjoy the activity.
- Important to establish so that all participants know what is expected of them when playing a particular sport or engaging in exercise and physical activities/following role-model behaviour.
- So that behaviour is socially acceptable (in a particular culture)/to show good control.
- To show respect to those around you/well mannered/to care about the well-being of others/sportsmanship/good etiquette/respect.
- To not be disqualified/sent off/fined.
- To not let your team-mates down/to avoid giving your team a bad name.

3. b *(1 mark)*

## 5. The components of fitness and a healthy, balanced lifestyle, p.12

1. a *(1 mark)*
2. c *(1 mark)*
3. *(4 marks)*

- Flexibility: Able to stretch/prevents injury/improves speed/power – for example, to be able to perform skills in gymnastics or to be able to stretch for things in everyday life.
- Muscular endurance: To be able to lift or carry effectively for a long time or to be able to keep going with strength activities for a long period of time – for example, to be able to carry out repetitive tasks without tiring or to be able to finish an exercise programme for one hour.

## 6. The importance of the warm-up and cool-down, p.14

1. *(5 marks)*

- Raise pulse/heart rate by jogging or running to raise pulse.
- Increasing body/muscle temperature.
- Stretching for at least 20–30 seconds per main muscle group/per stretch.
- Stretching main muscle groups/those muscles specifically going to be used; using flexibility or stretching exercises.
- Steady breathing/keeping control/calm.
- Including exercise movements that emulate the 'real game' situation.
- Using skill drills/practising techniques/shots.
- Incremental work rate in warm-up/start slow and build up work ready for game/competition.
- Mentally preparing for the activity.

2. *(5 marks)*

A suitable description of a cool-down to include steady jogging/running/exercise and stretching.

It is important because:

- it speeds up/removes or gets rid of lactic acid or waste products.
- it decreases risk of injury or pulling a muscle.
- it decreases the risk of muscle soreness or cramp or stiffness.
- it prevents blood pooling.
- it prevents feeling tired or fatigued.
- it *gradually* decreases heart rate/blood pressure/maintains blood pressure.
- it *gradually* decreases body temperature.
- it *gradually* decreases breathing rate.
- it stops you feeling dizzy or faint or sick.
- it has psychological benefits or makes you calm down or lowers anxiety.

3. a *(1 mark)*

4. d *(1 mark)*

## 7. The characteristics of skilful movement, p.16

1. b *(1 mark)*

2. *(4 marks)*

- Efficient/economic/effortless
- Pre-determined/knows what is needed/what they are doing/goal directed/knowing how you are going to win/predictable
- Consistent
- Coordinated/controlled
- Confident
- Fluent/flowing/smooth
- Successful/follows technical model/more likely to beat an opponent
- Learned.

3. *(3 marks)*

- Efficiency/economic/effortless (for example, no wasted energy when hitting a ball in tennis).
- Pre-determined (for example, the gymnast knows her routine well before she starts).
- Coordinated – (for example, the footballer can jump and do a 'bicycle kick' successfully).
- Fluent/fluid/smooth (for example, the rugby player picks up the ball and passes in one flowing movement).
- Aesthetic (for example, the netball player shoots the ball using the correct technique that looks good).
- Being creative (for example, a footballer can disguise a pass).
- Successful/good technique (for example, a basketballer shows the correct shooting technique.
- Controlled (for example, a volleyball player controls a dig).
- Perform at speed (for example, a netball player passes with speed).
- Consistent (for example, a tennis player serves well every time she serves).

- Learned (for example, a trampolinist learns a new technique of somersault).
- Confident (for example, a cricketer shows confidence when playing a forward defensive shot).

## 8. Performance and outcome goals, p.18

1. b *(1 mark)*

2. b *(1 mark)*

3. *(6 marks)*

**Performance:**

- Performance relates to techniques/skills/how well you carry out skills. A suitable practical example is setting a goal to improve your forehand in tennis.
- Performance also relates to strategies/making the right decision at the right time, for example, set a goal to work on when to use the dummy pass in rugby.

**Outcome:**

- Outcome relates to the result of an activity, for example one's goal might be to win all the remaining home games in netball.
- Outcome also relates to how others rate your performance/how you are judged, for example, scoring a high mark for the gymnastic floor routine.

**Other factors:**

- Both type of goals can be motivating – for example, setting a goal to improve your personal best in athletics.
- Make your goals relevant/achievable – for example, in netball trying to score 9 out of 10 shots/goals.

## 9. Assessing the body's readiness for exercise, p.20

1. c *(1 mark)*

2. *(3 marks)*

- Fitness tests
- Body mass index/BMI
- Cardiovascular tests/Cooper's 12-minute run test/Multi-stage fitness test/checking heart-rate recovery
- Strength test/grip dynamometer test
- Muscular endurance/sit-up test
- Speed test/30m sprint test
- Agility/balance/coordination test
- Flexibility test/sit and reach test
- Power test/standing broad jump
- Questionnaire questioning about how they feel
- Visual assessment/do they look ready for exercise?

3. *(4 marks)*

- To indicate how fit they are.
- To recognise if they are overweight.
- Indicates how much exercise should be done/is needed in an exercise programme.
- This is a measurement of your weight (kg)/weigh them, divided by your height (m)/measure their height.

- Compare score to national norms/check against BMI chart/graph.
- Age/body composition is another variable/factor.
- If there is a high score then this means they are overweight/this is undesirable/a BMI greater than 25 indicates being overweight.
- A score between 18–25 is more desirable.
- A score over 40 is a serious health risk.
- A score 30 indicates obesity (in adults)/health risk.
- A BMI should not be the only measure for readiness to exercise.
- It should not be used to assess those who are pregnant/highly trained athletes.

## 10. Components of a healthy diet and characteristics of a healthy lifestyle, p.24

1. *(4 marks)*

**Vitamins**

- Prevent infections/illness.
- Help to produce energy.
- Help with metabolism/with body systems working effectively.

**Minerals**

- Needed for strong/healthy bones/teeth/skin.
- Essential for blood/helps with carrying oxygen.
- Essential for effective growth/development.

2. b *(1 mark)*

3. a *(1 mark)*

4. c *(1 mark)*

5. *(6 marks)*

- Eating the right amount (for energy expended)/eating according to how much you work/exercise.
- Have an appropriate portion size/not too much or too little food.
- Eating breakfast.
- Having sufficient water.
- Limited or non-use of alcohol.
- Approximately 50 per cent carbohydrates.
- Not too much sugar.
- Not too much salt.
- About 30–35 per cent fats/not too many (saturated) fats.
- About 15–20 per cent protein.
- Fibre/roughage intake sufficient.
- Sufficient minerals.
- Sufficient vitamins.
- Plenty of fruit/vegetables/at least five a day.
- Variety of foods/different food groups.

6. b *(1 mark)*.

## 11. General factors affecting performance and participation, p.28

1 *(4 marks)*

- Causes muscle weakness/harder to do things.
- Performance/speed/stamina/participation decreases (give an example of this decrease).
- Loss/lack of energy available/tiredness/low blood sugar/dizziness/nausea/faintness.
- Causes weight loss that may decrease strength/mobility/power.
- May feel embarrassed/low self-esteem.
- More illness/disease.
- Not having a healthy diet/loss of vitamins/minerals.
- Slows growth and development/weaker bones/more prone to injury.
- Slows recovery after exercise/after illness.
- Loss of motivation/lethargy/not alert/slow reactions.

2. c *(1 mark)*

3. *(4 marks)*

**Positive effects:**

- Can increase levels of performance/make one play better.
- More strength/builds muscle.
- Have more energy/can last longer/recover faster/more stamina/train at greater intensity/be fitter.
- Masks injury so one can endure injury/pain better.
- Increased speed/power.
- Increase in red blood cells/increase in oxygen availability.
- Reduce weight.
- Control anxiety/calms/relaxes.
- Lowers heart rate.
- Speeds up reactions/more alert/better concentration.
- Increases confidence.

**Negative effects:**

- Withdrawal symptoms if you stop.
- High blood pressure.
- Skin problems/acne.
- More aggression/rage.
- Addiction/you can't help but take them/a habit.
- Anxiety/depression/lower self-esteem.
- Can lead to being banned/fined/disqualified.
- Labelled as a cheat by others/others have low opinion of you.
- Can affect gender characteristics: males get female characteristics/females get male characteristics.
- Heart disease/blood clots/kidney and internal organ damage/poor health/death.
- Infections/AIDS.

4. *(4 marks)*

- May have physical/health difficulties that limit performance/lack of strength/power/co-ordination/prone to illness.
- May have mental/cognitive difficulties that limit performance.

- No/lack of suitable activities on offer/not many teams available.
- No/lack of specialist coaches/teachers.
- Lack of role models.
- Limited access to facilities/no wheelchair access/no ramps.
- Difficulties in transport/getting to use facilities.
- Limited specialist equipment/resources for disability participation.
- Others may discriminate against participation/getting picked on.
- Feeling of helplessness/lack of confidence/low self-esteem/embarrassment.
- Lack of money.

## 12. Indicators of health and well-being, p.32

**1.** *(3 marks)*
- Satisfaction with life/contentment.
- Frequency of positive feelings/feeling good or positive/looking on the bright side/happy/positive mental health.
- The frequency of activities/how active you are/getting involved in sport/exercise.
- How well you look after yourself/drugs /alcohol/diet/following a balanced, healthy lifestyle.
- Self-pride/self-esteem/having a place in society.
- How lonely you are/amount and quality of friendships/having support from others/socially healthy.
- Health-screening aspects/levels of blood pressure/cholesterol/BMI.
- Confidence/levels stress/anxiety.
- Fitness tests.
- Good sleep patterns.
- Questionnaires.
- Not being poor/in poverty.

2. c *(1 mark)*
3. b *(1 mark)*
4. *(4 marks)*
- You have more space to participate.
- It is easy to go for walks or to jog.
- You feel less overcrowded or claustrophobic.
- It gives a varied experience/varied landscape or environment.
- It's pleasant or uplifting or is good to look/aesthetically pleasing.
- It provides an escape from pollution or urban litter, etc.

## 13. Methods of exercise and training, p.34

1. d *(1 mark)*
2. c *(1 mark)*

## 14. Levels of participation, p.36

1. a *(1 mark)*
2. c *(1 mark)*
3. b *(1 mark)*
4. *(4 marks)*

- The recommended amount of exercise is one hour every day for children and 30 minutes at least five times a week for adults. About one-third hit the target. A fifth only exercised once a month or less.
- the five most popular physical activities are:
  Walking (46 per cent)
  Swimming (35 per cent)
  Keep fit/yoga – including aerobics and dance exercise (22 per cent)
  Cycling (19 per cent)
  Cue sports - billiards, snooker and pool (17 per cent).
- Men are more likely than women to participate in sports activities – about 51 per cent of men compared with 36 per cent of women.
- 44% of men and 31% of women who participate in at least one activity (excluding walking and darts) belong to a sports club.
- In general, participation rates decrease with age.

## 15. Reasons for participation, p.38

1. d *(1 mark)*
2. *(3 marks)*
- Health-related/less likely to be ill.
- Physical reasons:fitness/weight control/more energy.
- Well-being/mental reasons/stress relief.
- Image.
- Enjoyment.
- Social/friendship/meeting friends.
- As a hobby/something to do/to keep active.
- To experience competition.
- To develop skills/to get better at the activity to perform everyday tasks better.
- To copy role models/significant others/parents/friends.
- As a vocation/profession/as a job/for money/tangible rewards.

3. a *(1 mark)*

## 16. Reasons for non-participation, p.40

1. c *(1 mark)*
2. *(6 marks)*
- Poor health/injury.
- Disability.
- Do not enjoy physical activities/had negative experiences at school with physical activities/PE/can't be bothered/lazy.
- Other competing interests/social life/other hobbies/computer games/(part time) work too time-consuming/no time.
- Discrimination by others.
- Pressure from peers not to participate/no friends to participate with.
- Cultural/religious reasons/frowned upon by others.
- Lack of confidence/self-esteem/feel embarrassed.
- Lack of role model/parental support/encouragement.

- Few opportunities/facilities/access (for disabled) lack of transport.
- Lack of money/equipment.
- Not compulsory (after 16).

3.  b *(1 mark)*

## 17. Specific social, cultural and locational reasons affecting participation, p.42

1.  *(4 marks)*

**Positive**

- Give personal support/help/advice.
- Attend/watch/support events/give transport/lifts to venue.
- Show positive role models that are active/show an interest in physical activities.
- Give financial support/provide/buy equipment.

**Negative**

- Show little support/interest/they are indifferent.
- Poor role models/do not participate themselves.
- Give no financial support.
- Stop/obstruct participation.

2.  c *(1 mark)*

3.  b *(1 mark)*

## 18. School Key Processes and influences on participation, p.44

**1.** *(6 marks)*

**Evaluation:**

- Observe/watch performance/use video.
- Time/take measurements of performance/stats.
- Identify strengths and weaknesses.
- Assess against previous targets.
- Use peer assessments.
- Self-assessments.
- Fitness tests/measurements.

**Improvements**:

- Improve by goal (SMART) setting/performance/outcome goals/telling them what's wrong.
- Encourage/support/reward/raise confidence.
- Punish or withdraw reward if failure.
- Show role models/good technical models.
- Set (progressive) practices/teach skills/techniques.
- Monitor/record progress.
- Educate them/give them more knowledge (about how to improve).
- Improve fitness.
- Improve psychological readiness/mental rehearsal/focus.

2.  c *(1 mark)*

3.  d *(1 mark)*

4.  d *(1 mark)*

## 19. Pathways for involvement in physical activity, p.46

1.  d *(1 mark)*

2.  *(6 marks)*

- Participating (regularly) in activity.
- In PE lessons/NC classes by participating/coaching/officiating.
- Extra-curricular activities/clubs/school teams.
- Member of external sports teams/exercise clubs.
- Coaching/teaching/leading new skills.
- Officiating/judging in a physical activity.
- Starting off at basic level of activities/other roles.
- Refinement of skills/getting help and advice/ being coached/practising.
- Getting to the next tier/level/representing county/moving up the performance pyramid.
- Developing physical health/fitness/following a healthy lifestyle.
- Volunteering to help or get involved.
- As a career/professional.
- Getting qualifications/scholarship.

3.  c *(1 mark)*

## 20. Learning skills, p.48

1.  a *(1 mark)*

2.  *(6 marks)*

- Practice/rehearsal.
- Through trial and error/having a go/learn by doing.
- Via a demonstration/visual guidance/modelling.
- Watching and copying others: observation learning.
- Watching videos/reading books.
- Learning is more likely if others are significant/role models.
- Being coached/taught/verbal guidance.
- Feedback from others.
- Knowledge of results/performance.
- Understanding what you need to learn.
- (Operant) conditioning.
- Being praised/reinforcement.

3.  d *(1 mark)*

4.  c *(1 mark)*

## 21. Feedback and motivation, p.50

1.  a *(1 mark)*

2.  b *(1 mark)*

3.  *(6 marks)*

- Encourage them to try something different or novel/to bring variety into life/to let them have a go/experience officiating.
- Show, teach or coach them in how to officiate.
- Give praise.
- Give rewards/badges.
- Telling them can make money.

- Telling they can gain qualifications.
- Telling them that this is a way they can get involved in an activity even though they may not be a very good practitioner of it themselves.
- Show them role models.

## 22. Goal setting, p.52

1. *(6 marks)*

**What**

- **S –** Specific activity to your needs.
- **M –** Measurable – goals need to be assessed to see how well you are doing.
- **A –** Achievable/agreed – goals must be within your reach/capabilities or they can be agreed with your teacher/coach.
- **R –** Realistic/recorded – goals must not be too challenging or you will fail, or they should be recorded so that you can refer back to them to see how you are getting on.
- **T –** Time phased – goals should be planned to be achieved over a period of time.

**Why**

- To get better/increase/optimise performance/to keep fit.
- To ensure participation continues/keep exercising or training/ensure exercise adherence.
- To control anxiety/stress.
- To motivate and enthuse and to gain satisfaction/enjoyment.

2. a *(1 mark)*
3. c *(1 mark)*

## 23. The skeletal system, p.54

1. c *(1 mark)*
2. d *(1 mark)*
3. *(5 marks)*

- Shape/support – for example, to protect internal organs.
- Blood cell (red) production – for example, to enable us to have energy.
- Mineral production/storage – for example, to keep us fit and healthy.
- Protection – for example, to avoid injury.
- To be able to move/keep moving/being mobile – for example, to be able to participate in physical exercise/acts as muscle attachment.
- Leverage.

## 24. Joints, p.56

1. *(3 marks)*

- It lubricates the joint.
- Thus protecting (cartilage).
- It ensures smooth/unobstructed/efficient movement and prevents friction.
- It is secreted into the joint by the synovial membrane, for example, the knee joint.

- It nourishes the cartilage.
- It helps to stabilise the joint.

2. d *(1 mark)*
3. a *(1 mark)*

## 25. Muscles and movement, p.58

1. a *(1 mark)*
2. *(5 marks)*

**(Any two major muscle groups)**

- Deltoids
- Trapezius
- *Latissimusdorsi*
- Pectorals
- Biceps
- Triceps
- Abdominals.

**(Explain how activity can keep muscles healthy)**

- Makes them stronger/bigger/hypertrophy.
- Less likely to strain/injury.
- Good blood/oxygen supply.
- Increase tolerance to lactic acid/tire less easily.
- Can keep going/helps (muscular) endurance.

3. c *(1 mark)*

## 26. Tendons and the effects of lactic acid, p.60

1. b *(1 mark)*
2. a *(1 mark)*
3. *(4 marks)*

- Produced because of lack of oxygen.
- After prolonged/hard high-intensity exercise.
- Causes fatigue/may cause us to stop.
- Can hurt/be painful.

## 27. Mental preparation, p.62

1. *(5 marks)*

- Keeping calm
- Mentally rehearsing or focusing
- Relaxing
- Being more confident
- Not criticising others
- Positive thinking
- Having empathy
- Showing sportsmanship
- Usng imagery
- Controlling anger.

2. b *(1 mark)*
3. *(4 marks)*

- Relaxes you – *Practical example, controlling anxiety in a tennis game.*
- Keeps you calm/'chilled'/lowers arousal – *Practical example, calms you down before performing a gymnastics floor routine.*

- Therefore you do not get carried away/over-excited/less angry – *Practical example, less angry when someone fouls you in hockey.*
- Can make decisions more effectively – *Practical example, a cricket captain can set a field calmly and effectively.*
- Less likely to be physically abusive/violent – *Practical example, will not retaliate if punched in rugby.*
- Less likely to make inflammatory comments – *Practical example, no back-chat to ref in football.*
- Being able to see other people's points of view/weigh things up more rationally – *Practical example, you can see why another player in netball is angry in netball because you have fouled her.*
- Will not miss important cues/hearing the whistle/officials' decisions that might lead to foul play – *Practical example, being focused in basketball will enable you to react quickly to referee decisions.*
- More likely to show etiquette, which may lead to less stress – *Practical example, in golf letting someone through who may be a quicker player.*

4. *(4 marks)*
- Improves performance/enables tactical or strategic decision making.
- Helps to control emotions/motivates you.
- Helps relaxing/coping with stress/concentrating.
- Helps to focus/selective attention.
- Able to visualise/use imagery.
- Quicker reactions/responses/decision making.
- Helps to raise confidence/self-esteem.
- Enables fair play.

## 28. Short-term effects of exercise, p.64

1. b *(1 mark)*
2. d *(1 mark)*
3. *(3 marks)*
- Increase in heart/pulse rate.
- Increase in cardiac output/more blood pumped out per minute.
- Increase in stroke volume/increase in blood (pumped out per beat).

4. *(3 marks)*
- Increase in tidal volume.
- Increase in minute volume.
- Increase in breathing rate.

## 29. Long-term effects of exercise, p.66

1. d *(1 mark)*
2. *(5 marks)*
- The elasticity of muscles improves. *Practical example: stretching during warm-ups and cool downs/regular exercise such as walking and swimming can help to stretch muscle.*
- Muscle use can build muscle/hypertrophy/build more fibres/strengthens muscles. *Practical examples: regular walking/running/gardening/training/exercise classes.*

- Variety of exercise will maintain and develop a good range of muscles. *Practical examples: varied trained methods/walking and swimming.*
- Less likely for injury/increase in muscle tone. *Practical examples: regular exercise maintains health/positivity.*
- Healthy eating can ensure the right nutrients for muscle growth and repair. *Practical examples: eating a balanced diet/including vitamins and mineral/regular meals with protein.*
- Resting muscles/recuperation after injury can help to maintain and heal. *Practical examples: resting during and after exercise.*
- Rehabilitation/specialist therapy/physiotherapy/massage can help to maintain and develop. *Practical examples: if pulled a muscle then go to doctor to be referred/go to physio for treatment/use rehab exercises.*
- Increase in speed. *Practical examples: can run faster/more efficiently.*
- Increase power. *Practical examples: can lift/do physical work more effectively.*
- More endurance. *Practical examples: can keep going/not get tired.*

3. a *(1 mark)*
4. *(4 marks)*
- Increase in size (of muscle fibres)/hypertrophy of muscles.
- Increase in strength (of muscle fibres)/tone/power.
- Increase in muscular endurance/last longer.
- Increase in flexibility(of muscle)/elasticity.
- Increased tolerance to lactic acid.
- Increased rate of removal of lactic acid.
- Greater potential for energy production/more energy available.
- Size/number of mitochondria increased.
- Increase in myoglobin (within muscle cells).
- Increase in capillaries in muscles/more oxygen/ haemoglobin to (working) muscles.
- Helps prevent injury/helps recovery from injury.
- Causes injury/strains/damage/can decrease mobility.

## 30. Exercise and training principles, p.68

1. b *(1 mark)*
2. d *(1 mark)*
3. *(3 marks)*
- **Overload:** Work harder than normal/puts body under stress/adaptation will follow/comes about by increasing frequency/intensity/duration. *For example, lifting heavier weights.*
- **Specificity:** Training should be particular/relevant to needs (examiners will not accept specific on its own without explanation)/relevant energy system used/ relevant muscle groups used. *For example, choosing main muscle groups used in activity to train for strength.*
- **Progression:** (Gradually) becomes more difficult/ demanding/challenging/once adapted then more demands on body. *For example, doing more repetitions of sprints at each training session.*

- **Reversibility:** Performance/fitness can deteriorate if training/exercise stops/decreases. *For example, if you stop endurance training your stamina will reduce in time.*

## 31. Aerobic and anaerobic exercise and training, p.70

1. a *(1 mark)*
2. c *(1 mark)*
3. a *(1 mark)*
4. *(4 marks)*

### Aerobic exercise

- This is when the body is working **with** the presence of oxygen.
- It is a continuous, steady state (sub-maximal) training.
- The rhythmic exercise of aerobics is an example as are continuous swimming or jogging, and these are all good for aerobic fitness.
- This low-intensity exercise must take place over a long period of time from 20 minutes to 2 hours.
- The intensity of this exercise should be 60–80 per cent of your maximum heart rate.

### Anaerobic exercise

- This is when the body is working **without** the presence of oxygen.
- This type of training involves high-intensity work.
- This type of activity can only be carried out for a short amount of time.

## 32. Potential hazards, p.72

1. a *(1 mark)*
2. c *(1 mark)*
3. b *(1 mark)*
4. *(5 marks)*

- Poorly maintained equipment.
- Equipment that can be obstacles/gets in the way/is improperly housed.
- Falling or unstable equipment/weights.
- Floor slippery/rough/uneven/dirty.
- Litter/discarded objects/bags.
- Improper use of the equipment/lifting too many weights/overdoing the exercise.
- Electrical equipment.
- Crowded area/too many people or other participants.
- Clothing/improper footwear.
- Door handles/radiators/fixtures and fittings (other than activity equipment).
- Air conditioning/heating problems/too hot/too cold.

## 33. Reducing the risks, p.74

1. b *(1 mark)*
2. a *(1 mark)*
3. *(5 marks)*

- Ensure the activity is supervised/qualified instructor/go with someone else.

- Correct clothing/footwear/shoes/properly fastened clothing/fits well.
- Personal protective equipment/the right equipment.
- Risk assessment.
- Follow health and safety procedures.
- Check equipment for faults.
- Take the climate/weather/environment/surfaces into account (when planning/continuing)/keep track of where you are.
- Ensure activities are suitable for the age/ability/experience of the participants.
- Lift and carry equipment correctly.
- Exercise/compete at appropriate level/don't overdo it.
- Warm-up/cool-down/stretching exercises.
- Correct technique/skills.
- Take telephone/tell someone where you are going.
- Cover any cuts/abrasions with a plaster.

## 34. Effects of media and sponsorship, p.76

1. c *(1 mark)*
2. c *(1 mark)*
3. *(6 marks)*

- Wide/intense/regular coverage of sport on TV.
- Internet/websites encourage interest and therefore participation.
- Press/written media has extensive coverage of sport.
- Encourages general interest in sport/physical activities/exercise.
- Gives ideas about new/novel activities.
- Promotes/educates about benefits to health/well-being.
- Show consequences of low activity levels.
- Can inform about how to participate.
- Can inform about where to participate.
- Entertains and therefore attracts participation (Wimbledon and tennis).
- Media attracts sponsorship/funding to clubs/individuals that may then encourage more participation.
- Can lead to rule changes.
- Can lead to events being on at different times/days, thereby affecting participation.

### Negative aspects

- Negative view that media may link activity to undesirable factors for some people/alcohol/competitiveness, etc.
- Can give activities a bad name.
- Coverage can be limiting/only some sports represented.
- Over-emphasis on male/able-bodied sport.
- Can encourage aggression.
- Can encourage nationalism/prejudice/jingoism.

## 35 Local and national provision, p.78

1. *(3 marks)*

- The BOA selects Team GB/selects the best.
- Helps prepare and acclimatise before the Olympics.

- Organises visits to the host city prior to the Olympic Games.
- Has an (exclusive) preparation camp.
- With the best facilities for Team GB/places to stay.
- Provide some (top-class) equipment.
- Provides top-class facilities at the British Olympic Training Centre/places to train (Austria).
- Runs programmes that assist athletes throughout their training.
- Help with funding/providing discounts at national and local sports centres.
- Helping athletes find jobs (which fit around their training and competition).
- Help with travel.

2. c *(1 mark)*
3. *(3 marks)*

*For example:*

- FA – Football
- LTA – Tennis
- ASA – Swimming, etc.

## 36. Government initiatives, p.80

**1.** *(6 marks)*

- Healthy Living programme – *aimed at tackling barriers of limited parental awareness.*
- 5 A Day message/5 (+) fruit and veg each day – *Fruit and veg of different colours provide a wide range of vitamins, minerals, fibre and healthy antioxidants, which can help to protect the body throughout life.*
- Walking to school/use of bikes to get to school – *Simple message, easy to understand/has little scientific standing but is known by many so very motivating.*
- Top Tips for Top Mums/advice to mothers – *Encourages parents across the country to share tips and ideas with*

*each other on how they get their children to eat more fruit and vegetables.*

- Promotion of healthy diets and physical activity in the run up to the 2012 Olympics/2012 initiatives for health.
- 'Change4Life' healthy lifestyles marketing initiative.
- Five Choices to help you stay healthy.
- You should not smoke/Do some regular physical activity/Eat a healthy diet/Try to lose weight if you are overweight or obese/Don't drink too much alcohol.
- 30 mins of moderate aerobic physical activity, on most days.
- Minimum of two sessions of muscle-strengthening activities per week (not on consecutive days).
- Children and teenagers should get at least one hour a day of moderate physical activity.

2. c *(1 mark)*

## 37. School influences, p.82

1. a *(1 mark)*
2. *(4 marks)*

- Raises awareness of positive reasons/health benefits of participation.
- Measures health/fitness.
- Educates about health and fitness.
- Helps to set goals for better health/fitness.
- School provides resources/(better) equipment that can be used by all.
- Encourages participation because of the practical element/you have to participate in practical activities to complete the course.
- Provides role models in the school/others want to copy successful pupils/others around you are motivated.

3. a *(1 mark)*

# Index